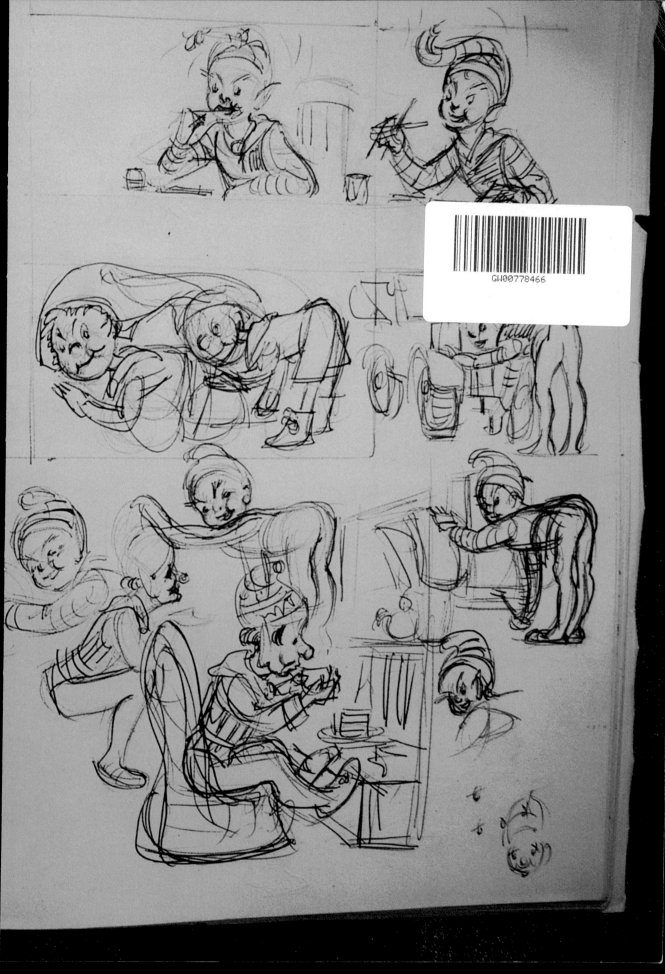

Inside front cover illustration: sketchbook pages "Run, Noddy, Run!" published in *Sunny Stories*, February 1952.
Inside back cover: "White Trousers", *Sunny Stories*, January 1952.

Published by Pomegranate Press,
Dolphin House, 51 St Nicholas Lane, Lewes, Sussex BN7 2JZ
pomegranatepress@aol.com
www.pomegranate-press.co.uk

ISBN: 978–1–907242–18–2

British Library Cataloguing-in-Publication Data.
A catalogue record for this book is available from the British Library

Printed and bound by Ashford Colour Press, Gosport, Hants PO13 0FW

A Brush with Enid Blyton

The life and work
of Marjorie L. Davies

Sally Varlow

ACKNOWLEDGEMENTS

This book would not have been possible without the generous support of Angie Clements Jenkins; and the kind assistance of Davydd Shaw, who gave permission to reproduce text and pictures from his book, *Marjorie Davies, An Appreciation*, and Jacquie Bravery, who supplied family photos and access to MLD's papers. I am also indebted to Tony Summerfield of the Enid Blyton Society for help with research and images from Enid Blyton's books and magazines; Alan Evison and Lesley Dunford for photographing artwork; Chailey Heritage Enterprise Centre for photographs; and David Arscott of Pomegranate Press for his careful handling of some less-than-perfect originals. But my biggest debt is to Marjorie, a dear friend for over 25 years.

Sally Varlow, April 2011

CONTENTS

Marjorie Louise Clements, c. 1927.

Marjorie Louise Davies was born on 5 June, 1906, in Hampstead, London, the third of five children, and the only daughter of Alfred and Louise Clements. Alfred had grown up in Hampstead and he and Louise made their home there on the edge of the heath, in the Vale of Health, at Laburnum Cottage. Not far away, at North Villa, lived Alfred's eldest brother John, his wife Clara and their son Bert.[1]

In 1908, when Marjorie was two, the Clements' happy family life was interrupted by tragedy when her four-year-old brother, Eric, was killed in a street accident. Louise had been walking along the High Street with her two eldest sons, Jack and Eric, pushing her fourth child, Con, in a pram, when a car mounted the kerb and fatally injured Eric. Louise never really recovered from this event, though it was not until several years later that she developed consumption (TB). Soon after Eric's death the family moved to Radlett in Hertfordshire, where John Clements and his family were now living, and there Louise's last child, Vic , was born.[2]

"Mother became ill when I was seven, and she died nine years later," Marjorie recalled,[3] indicating that Louise's illness was diagnosed towards the end of 1913, since she died in February 1924. Because of Louise's condition and current medical practice, it was considered best for her to be moved to a sanatorium near sea air, and the place chosen was The Home Sanatorium, West Southbourne in Hampshire, close to the seafront between Bournemouth and Christchurch harbour.

Every Saturday the children wrote to her and frequently travelled with their father, by train from Waterloo, to spend a couple of days visiting her and staying nearby. After tea in her room they would walk to the seafront and watch minesweepers out at sea and airships overhead, during the Great War of 1914–18 (World War I).

Following Louise's removal to Bournemouth, in 1914 Alfred decided that he and the children should live with his widowed sister, Emily Forster, and her son, Wally. Aunt Emily ran her large house, 49 Brondesbury Road, Kilburn, London, like a high-class boarding house, and the residents included Mab Kell, an army colonel, an old nanny to the former Kaiser, and Bridget the maid.

Despite the distress of her mother's illness, Marjorie's early years at the boarding house were happy ones. She was fond of her aunt and Bridget, and there were regular

Marjorie, c. 1909.

Louise Clements, c. 1920.

Alfred Clements, 1939.

visits to other members of the family. Her cousins Will and Doris Gent[4] lived close enough to be regular companions, and to join Marjorie and her brothers helping Alfred grow fruit and vegetables on the family's allotment, at weekends and after school.

Marjorie was getting on well at school and kept careful diary records of her school marks – usually top of the class or just a couple of marks below. Her diary for 1918 also records the nightly war-time air raids on London by German planes, heralded by sirens: "Had raid in evening. 'Take cover' at 10.15. 'All clear' at 1 o'clock." On 9 March there was the added excitement of seeing an "Airship and aeroplane dropped parachute".

With her father and brothers she paid visits to a nearby airfield, presumably Hendon five miles away, to see some of the planes used by the Royal Flying Corps. Cousin Wally had become a gunner with the British Expeditionary Force in France, and in January (1918) he was home for "14 days' leave from the Front". But on 25 March they learned that he was "wounded in leg and shell shock", and on 3 May he was still "in hospital in France on his birthday". Though the war was now entering its final months, a few nights later North London suffered yet another "Bad raid. 11.10 'Take cover' 2 o'clock 'All clear' came back 2.10 T.C. 2.30 A.C."

From her diary it is also clear that Marjorie was an avid reader, and some of her earliest books became life-long possessions, including *Jessica's First Prayer* by Hesba Stretton, in which she wrote her name and Brondesbury Road address in a round girlish hand; *The Motor Scout* by Herbert Strang, a gift "To Marjorie Clements from Dada"; and *What Katy Did Next*, inscribed "1st Sewing Prize – Awarded to Marjorie Clements".

It was only one of many awards. In December 1917, having moved on to Oakwood House School, Kilburn, she won a book on *Old Bow China* as a prize for drawing. The following year, on 31 October she received a volume of *Titian Masterpieces in Colour* for "Honour" and "1st Art Prize". This must have been first in her year group, as the same date saw her brother, Con, also winning a companion volume, *Bellini Masterpieces in Colour* as "1st Art Prize". At Christmas that year she received, "From Mum", *The Jolliest Term on Record*, by the popular girls' author Angela Brazil.

Marjorie had seen a lot of her mother in the preceding months and spent a three-week family holiday, from

August to September, staying near the sanatorium. Between daily visits to Louise, they enjoyed walking and bathing, picnicking on the beach and tram rides to Boscombe. To mark Louise's birthday, on 4 September, they took her to the cliffs. Ten days later they left and Marjorie and her brothers returned to school.

On the train back to London they watched German aeroplanes circling over London and in October there was still the odd Zeppelin in the sky. But on Sunday, 10 November: "Dada took us to Mall and saw 400 captured guns." The following day: "PEACE. Armistice signed by Germans." Within a week they were at Southbourne again, visiting Louise for the weekend.

But the war was not forgotten and a few years later, as she told Davydd Shaw,[5] she visited the battlefields in Flanders: "When she was about 18, Alfred took her there with Bridget, the maid, and I think Jack. Bridget greatly suffered from the death of her brother there, and it was hoped the visit to the grave and the battlefields might help her. The day her brother was killed, Bridget had collapsed on the stairs wailing, even though the telegram advising of his death only arrived several days later. Marjorie remembered seeing evidence of weapons and destruction of buildings and farmlands."[6] And among the many photographs she kept was a packet of small brown, undated, snapshots showing Alfred seated on the deck of a ferry at Boulogne; Alfred standing on a large field gun, labelled "Big Bertha – 25 mile range"; "German trenches and dugout 28 feet deep"; "Ramparts at Ypres"; rusting tanks and a ruined church.

In autumn 1920, still at school, Marjorie again won an Oakwood House "1st Art Prize", another book, titled *A Hero of Old France* by John Harrington Cox; and there was an extra reward – *Black Partridge* by Col. H.R Gordon, "From Dad, 28th October 1920, for good school work". As well as art lessons she was learning the piano and evidently played well, though her shyness at performing before an audience deterred her from taking part in school concerts. Out of school one of her chief pleasures was playing cricket with her brothers – a sport she followed keenly and knowledgeably for the rest of her life.

In 1923, on 15 October, she won her last school prizes: "1st Scripture prize", and as usual, "1st prize for art". Her obvious talent and early interest in art were attributed by Marjorie to her friendship with an artist neighbour named Florrie Twort. Another neighbour was the well-known cat artist and illustrator Louis Wain, who she remembered

Visiting World War I battlefields. Top to bottom: Alfred (left) on the ferry at Boulogne; Alfred on "Big Bertha"; German guns by the Cloth Hall, Ypres.

With three brothers, a love of cricket was essential.

Mab and Marjorie.

"as rather a sinister figure".[7] But it was a visiting art teacher at Oakwood House who contacted Alfred and told him he should take Marjorie and her portfolio to the principal of St Martin's Art School. Marjorie was accepted immediately and in 1923 began a full-time, three-year course, followed by part-time courses for several more years.

She had only been at art school a few months when, in February 1924, her mother finally succumbed to the illness that had kept her an invalid for the past 10 years. It seems, from books exchanged at Christmas 1923, that Aunt Emily's boarder, Mab Kell, had already formed a close relationship with Alfred's family. Marjorie's eldest brother, Jack, presented her with *The Day's Work* by Rudyard Kipling, signing it: "To Mab – wishing you every happiness and good luck in the New Year, from Jack". While Marjorie gave "Auntie Mab" another Kipling volume, *Barrack Room Ballads*, "with much love and best wishes from Marjorie, Christmas 1923."

Mabel Alice Kell[8] had qualified as a vocal music teacher in 1904 and as a PE teacher two years later. She was still teaching when the Clements first came to live at the boarding house, though after her marriage to Alfred, on 16 April, 1925, she would almost certainly have stopped working. Alfred now established a home of his own again, taking Mab and his children back to live on the edge of Hampstead Heath, at 9 Mackeson Road.

Mab's presence in the family was not entirely a happy one and it was generally understood later that after her marriage she did not really make the rest of the family very welcome.[9] This created a degree of sensitivity in Alfred's children, especially as her sister Violet married Marjorie's cousin, Bert Clements. For years Marjorie continued giving Mab books for birthdays and Christmas, with "best love" or "much love". And in the summer of 1927, shortly after her 21st birthday, she joined her father and step-mother on a lengthy car-tour of Devon, Cornwall and the Wye Valley, visiting every beauty spot from Land's End and Lamorna Cove to Tintern Abbey. But in later life Marjorie never mentioned Mab with particular affection, remembering instead the autocratic way Mab treated "a little Scottish girl called Maggie".[10] Margaret Casey, as she is named in Alfred's will, was first employed as the family's live-in domestic help, later became Alfred's housekeeper till his death, and subsequently spent lengthy periods in the 1970s, staying with Marjorie as her companion.[11]

By the time of her step-mother's arrival, however, Marjorie had much to occupy her away from home, as she had embarked on her second year at art school, travelling there daily from Mackeson Road.

At St Martins, then one of London's three leading art schools, together with the Slade and the Academy, Marjorie followed the full range of art training, including life painting, still life, calligraphy and drawing, but she showed particular talent as a portrait painter in oils, which she studied under William Bramley.

Portrait studies from Marjorie's student days, 1923–1927.

Rough proof detail from "Gnomes in the Kitchen", drawn for Arthur Mee's My Magazine, 1932.

WORK AND MARRIAGE, 1927–39

Having finished her full-time training at St Martin's, Marjorie began freelance work in and around London, "and soon obtained a number of portrait commissions, including painting the American ambassador's children. However, she found painting conditions difficult. Her shyness meant she did not feel comfortable making 'small talk' with her employers; and the dark and sometimes dingy libraries or drawing rooms in big old houses into which she was ushered to paint the lady of the house or her children, provided less than ideal conditions."[12] Furthermore, the rented studio she shared in the late 1920s with fellow student artist R.E. Jordan, at 38 Gunter Grove, Chelsea, was not good enough for portrait painting.

Instead, she began developing what would become her most successful art work: children's pictures, often highly detailed studies of small animals doing more-or-less human things, and always characterised by her sense of fun and inventiveness.

Her record book of commissions and work sold, meticulously kept for over 30 years, begins in February 1929 with two line drawings for the Religious Tracts Society's *Empire Annual for Girls*, illustrating a historical story, "Prudence and the Pirates". The same month she was working on drawings for a girls' adventure story for *The Guide*; and in June she finished a line drawing for *Bo-Peep's Bumper Book* 1929.

Her first full-colour plates appeared in *Blackie's Annual* 1931, swiftly followed by colour illustrations for Oxford University Press and a picture of rabbits titled "What a picnic!" for *Woman's Magazine*. In February that year Marjorie had been taken on by the influential Link Studio art agency, based in Great Queen Street, London. Through them she received a stream of 'blue-chip' commissions: not only the Blackie's work, but numerous jobs for Arthur Mee's monthly *My Magazine*. Mee was the foremost children's publisher of the day, creating 'posh' (Marjorie's description) periodicals, newspapers and books for young readers, using only the highest standard texts and artwork. Marjorie's illustrations for him were sometimes full colour, sometimes line drawing, but almost always featured rabbits: frolicking in the park, at the fair, preparing dinner, taking aeroplane trips and much more.

In the Chelsea studio, Marjorie and "Jordie", who "acted as our agent",[13] were also producing posters and pictorial advertisements. In 1931 she sold poster designs

Detail from "Frolics in the Park", for My Magazine, *1931.*

Poster designs for the Great Western Railway, 1931.

to Great Western Railways for their campaigns promoting trips to the countryside, "Ramble and be Fit", and tickets for passengers' dogs, earning five guineas and £10 respectively. The dogs' tickets promotion bore the slogan "Don't leave me with strangers" and offered everyone buying "7-day Holiday Season Tickets a weekly season ticket for their dogs at the special rate of 5/- [thus enabling] holidaymakers to enjoy the company of their dogs on daily outings at an exceedingly cheap rate." It was a campaign that would have touched the heart of anyone like Marjorie, who adored dogs and later owned a succession of spaniels.

On 15 January, 1932, Jordan wrote to the publicity manager at J. Lyons and Co, Cadby Hall, Kensington, chasing up a drawing Marjorie had submitted. Her roughs and snapshots show a team of rabbits mixing, baking and packaging Lyons Swiss Rolls. The following day the manager replied, to R. E. Jordan Esq: "I am afraid I now have sufficient drawings in stock for our present Swiss Rolls series." Yet it wasn't a complete brush-off. "I will endeavour to fix an appointment at a later date," he added.

Who Jordan was is not entirely clear. Among her books Marjorie kept a copy of Kipling's *Plain Tales from the Hills*, inscribed, "To Dearest Marjorie with love from Jordie, Xmas 1931"; and her photographs included a packet of prints marked "Jordie's film of Mersea trip 25.9.32."

During 1932 Marjorie was also attempting to sell flower paintings, and supplied six striking studies of roses, marigolds, chrysanthemums, anemones, Chinese lanterns and tulips to the well-known Palser Gallery in King Street, St James's. It was a thrill, she said, to walk down King Street and see one in the window,[14] but only two were sold and she withdrew the rest the following year.

By autumn that year she had given up the Chelsea studio and the Link was corresponding with her at 9 Mackeson Road. On 12 September they wrote returning "two rough sketches which we would like you to finish up in two colours (blue and red) the same size as usual. Our clients are very interested in these drawings, but they do not buy from rough sketches. Although this is in the nature of a speculative job, we think they will both be sold." According to her records, they *were* sold, and "Gnomes Market (blue and red), Gnomes Railway Station (ditto)" appeared in *Puck's Annual*. It was just one of the

From the top: detail from sketch for a Lyons Swiss Roll advertisement, 1932; detail from "Rough Proof", c. 1932; "Roses" for the Palser Gallery, 1932.

popular children's annuals she worked for, together with *Pip, Squeak and Wilfred Annual, Warne's, Dean's, Pearson's* and *Hulton's*.

The following January her regular contact at the Link, Vernon Tovey, wrote to tell her: "I have parted company with the Link Studios, and have once more set up business on my own account. Since I was responsible for selling most of your work through the Link I shall be glad to have an opportunity of doing further business with you." Marjorie, however, was not about to leave the agency and allow him to represent her, no matter how much he felt she was obliged to him.

It was probably a very wise decision. The Link continued passing her valuable commissions and in July forwarded her the first of many jobs for the *Daily Mail* and *Sunday Dispatch*. Such work for national newspapers was always "Urgent" and required the artist to submit both the story line and pictures for a "seven picture adventure story", or a "vertical strip" cartoon.

In the circulation battle then raging between national

'Chinese lanterns' (right), displayed in the Palser Gallery, 1932, were a favourite subject often returned to and used (above) in her Christmas card for 2004.

Cartoon strips for the Daily Mail, *1932.*

daily papers one popular weapon was cartoon strips for very young readers. The *Daily Mirror* courted them with "Pip, Squeak and Wilfred",[15] so the *Daily Mail* fought back with "Rosebud and Willow", a pretty fairy and her pixie friend whose adventures were told in three tiny pictures each Saturday.

On 31 July the Link forwarded her a request for initial sketches: two strips of "Rosebud and Willow"; similar cartoons about two gnomes called "Timothy and Titus"; plus pictures titled "A Busy Day on the Farm" and "Edward Makes Himself Unpopular" – all to be completed "Soon as possible". Edward the elephant

Final sketches, *"Timothy & Titus"*, Daily Mail, *1932*.

upsetting a group of young rabbits, squirrels and mice by jumping into their swimming pool duly appeared in the *Sunday Dispatch* on 20 August. The farmyard scene, showing five naughty bunnies causing chaos among hens, pigs and horses, was published a week later.

Meanwhile, on 3 August, only four days after their previous request, the Link was asking for two of her suggested "Rosebud and Willow" strips to be worked up. On 19 August her picture-story of the two characters hiding inside foxglove flowers to escape from "a big hungry bird who thought they were butterflies" was printed; and a week later they were sailing across a pond in a water-lily boat. On the 23rd, the Link requested a rough of a "Snow Scene" to be done by Thursday 25th; and the following day they asked her to produce "At once" a picture titled "Bunniville on Sea", which was published in the *Dispatch* on Sunday, 3 September. They also wanted three more ideas for strips of "Rosebud and Willow".

On 4 September they returned one of her roughs to be worked up to finished art work. On the 6th they wanted "three more roughs . . . at your early convenience". Five days later they asked her to "kindly finish up the enclosed two 'Rosebud and Willow' and let us have the same as soon as possible."

It was a punishing schedule, but clearly the Link knew they could rely on her to come up with cartoons the newspapers would like. And on each Saturday in September the two little figures appeared playing hide-and-seek in a flower; creating a hammock out of a spider's web; summoning two birds to rescue Willow from the end of a flyaway kite; and earning some honey from a grateful bee who they had released from another web.

Ideas and sketches streamed off Marjorie's drawing board: Rosebud and Willow turning a matchbox into a cart for a tearful young pixie; hoisting a baby mouse back into its nest; making a mouse's pram out of an acorn shell; and frightening a frog with a pair of scissors disguised as a heron's beak. Not all of her ideas were accepted without amendments and on one occasion the first rough was returned marked "Idea OK, too muddled". Nonetheless, her altered version was published.

Whether "Timothy and Titus" and "Lop-Ear and Bob-Tail" – another roughly sketched strip submitted through the Link – ever appeared is uncertain; but a single picture of a watermill, surrounded by ducks, hens, sheep, cows, swallows and children was published by the *Sunday*

Dispatch on 10 September. Her last known published "Rosebud and Willow" cartoons appeared on 7 October. The paper had decided to rethink the format and on 12 September the Link sent her a hasty post-card instructing her to "hold up the Rosebud and Willow drawings, as the size is being altered. I will let you know the new sizes as soon as I here [*sic*] from the customer." In the mean time, plenty of commissions from other publications came her way through the Link, including a series of six drawings: Elves greeting . . ; Children and Toadstools; Children playing; Hallow Evening; Knight and Dragon; and Little Red Riding Hood. And among her sketchbooks, other rough cartoons, in larger format than "Rosebud and Willow", show her working on a story about a rabbit family out for a picnic, and another about a family of bees.

The postcard in October that advised her of changes to "Rosebud and Willow" was sent to 45 Devonshire Street, Regent's Park. It was then an unlikely part of London in which to rent a studio and it may be the temporary 'digs' she is believed to have moved into while her father and Mab were moving out of London to their first home in Hertfordshire. Exactly when Marjorie joined them at the new house, Kildare in Rectory Road, Rickmansworth, is not clear. During the summer and late autumn of 1933 she had been giving occasional watercolour lessons, at 12/- an hour, to "Miss Horton at Denham" – a short bus-ride from Rickmansworth, but a more difficult journey from Regent's Park.

She was certainly living at Kildare by the following spring when she received a commission which resulted in some of the finest colour plates she ever produced for children. Still aged only 27, she was given one of the most sought-after jobs in children's literature: illustrating a new edition of Lewis Carroll's classic tales *Alice's Adventures in Wonderland* and *Through the Looking Glass*.

On 9 May, 1934, the Link wrote to her: "We give below a copy of a letter we have today received from our clients. They are quite agreeable that you should have 3 weeks to execute this commission. With reference to our memo of the 4th inst. Regarding the commission to illustrate ALICE IN WONDERLAND we would like to include THROUGH THE LOOKING GLASS with this book. Would you therefore supply say, three illustrations from ALICE IN WONDERLAND and the remaining two from THROUGH THE LOOKING GLASS."

The customer was Hutchinson, a major publisher. Clearly they considered Marjorie could produce pictures

Initial sketch, "Edwards makes himself unpopular", Sunday Dispatch, 1933.

Sketch for "The March Hare and the Hatter were having tea ...", and final colour plate for "The Duchess was sitting on a three-legged stool, nursing a baby", Alice in Wonderland, *1934.*

good enough to compete with Sir John Tenniel's original illustrations, drawn in the 1860s. And having seen her initial pictures, their demands and urgency escalated. On 15 May the Link wrote again: "Our customers now want another 24 simple line illustrations for 'Alice in Wonderland' and 'Through the Looking Glass', one for each chapter. Each illustration is to be page width by 2 ½"– 3" deep and we should like the illustrations just a little bolder than the last lot you did for us. They also enquire how you are getting on with the others and would like to see any you have finished."

Enclosed was the formal agreement for the 24 line drawings, but only part of the manuscript, though the Link promised to forward the rest "as soon as it comes to hand".

In order to meet the difficult deadlines Marjorie's father acted as her courier, sending each finished or amended illustration to the Link in Holborn from his

offices at Crown House, in the Aldwych. There, on 31 May the Link wrote to him: "Dear Mr Clements, Very many thanks for sending the altered coloured plates this morning. Mr Williams thinks these will now be alright. With regard to the line drawing, your messenger did not wait so we were unable to send the message as requested but we think these would be better with just a little thicker lines."

Marjorie must have spent her 28th birthday, on 5 June, working round the clock to complete the pictures at Kildare, where the Link at last sent her the complete typescript for *Alice in Wonderland* and *Through the Looking Glass*. But now the customer wanted the "10 illustrations for the first part, Alice in Wonderland … and 10 illustrations for the second part, Alice Through the Looking Glass, to reduce", to approximately 2 ½ x 4 ½. "We also require one line end-paper size 9 ¼ x 14. We should be glad to have these drawings very quickly."

Rough sketch and colour plate for "The knight fell heavily on the top of his head", Through the Looking-Glass, *1934.*

21

(Right) Finished sketch for "The Queen never left off shouting 'Off with his head' ".

(Below) Preliminary sketch for "The White Rabbit was still in sight", Alice in Wonderland.

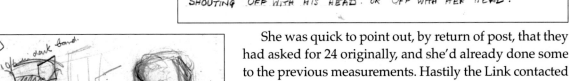

"ALL THE TIME THEY WERE PLAYING THE QUEEN NEVER LEFT OFF SHOUTING 'OFF WITH HIS HEAD!' OR 'OFF WITH HER HEAD!'"

She was quick to point out, by return of post, that they had asked for 24 originally, and she'd already done some to the previous measurements. Hastily the Link contacted the publisher and wrote back the following day assuring her: "any you have completed will be alright but for the remainder would you if possible choose the incidents they marked on the m/s we sent you yesterday and they can be done either the original size or the new size we sent you yesterday."

On 4 July the studio wrote again via her father's office, this time almost apologetically enquiring: "As our customers are very anxious to have the drawings, would you be kind enough to ask your father whether he would bring up tomorrow any you have finished … We are sorry to trouble you but we want if possible to satisfy our customers and keep them quiet for a few days until you have finished them all."

The finished book, a single volume combining *Alice in Wonderland* and *Through the Looking Glass*, handsomely bound in dark blue, was sufficiently admired to be reprinted in 1941 – a rare accolade given the paper shortage during World War II, which was then at its height. Marjorie, however, had some reservations about her illustrations. "I think [the figure of] Alice is awful," she told Enid Blyton's daughter, Imogen Smallwood. "I wish I could have done it after I had finished working for your mother. Then I could draw children."[16]

Rough sketch and colour plate for "If you don't hold your tongues, I'll pick you", Through the Looking-Glass.

(Opposite and left) Colour plate and finished sketch for " 'Call the first witness,' said the King"; (below) Rough sketch for " 'Ahem!' said the Mouse with an important air"; (below left) Initial sketch for "The Caterpillar took the hookah out of its mouth . . .", Alice in Wonderland.

What makes the speed and quality of her work remarkable is that before she began working on Alice she had already become a full-time member of the design studios at Shand Kydd, one of London's largest wallpaper makers. In October 1933 she recorded: "30/10/33 Nursery frieze (1st instal. Rabbits) submitted to Shand Kydd Ltd, Kentish Town (Mr Kydd, Mr Roland)." On 1 November they offered her a job, and she started work five days later at a weekly salary of £2.8.9d (less 1/8d insurance). "It was a prestige company with machine shops and print rooms, and six or eight artists working on designs in the studio – they were wonderful years," she recalled later.[17] Her job involved a variety of design and painting tasks, including mixing her own paint from pigments, and drawing room settings for the wallpaper sales catalogues. But most notable, and her favourites, were her illustrations for a children's nursery wallpaper frieze, based on Robert Browning's poem "The Pied Piper of Hamelin".

(Left) Pencil sketch for a colour plate c. 1930–34; (below) Proof from "A Bed-time Story" for Hutchinson's 1934; and proof detail from "Fairy Picnic" for Pearson's Annual, *1934.*

Even after the hectic Alice schedule was completed, Marjorie carried on freelancing while working with Shand Kydd. There was more colour-plate work for Hutchinson's and Pearson's – "Haymaking", "Fairy Picnic" and "Camping"; and in 1937/8 her full-plate picture "Dorothy's Dream" was eventually published in *Tiny Tots* annual.

Yet her busy working life did not prevent her from socialising with friends and fellow students. Among the closest was Madeleine Heath-Robinson, affectionately known as 'Smudge', who introduced Marjorie to her father and uncles, the well-known artists, Tom, William and Charles Heath-Robinson.

Two other particular friends were Anne, who Marjorie used to visit at the home of architect Clough Williams Ellis, where Anne's mother was housekeeper. And Violet Wilson, considered by Marjorie a very good artist, who later married her brother Con.[18]

(Opposite) Rough proofs from "The Pied Piper of Hamelin" children's wallpaper design for Shand Kydd, c. 1937;

In 1935 Marjorie was also married, to John Davies. She had met him at West Mersea, a favourite seaside destination on the Essex coast and, in her own words, he looked like, "a blonde god walking along".[19] Handsome he undoubtedly was, and they shared two great interests: antiques and sailing, especially around Mersea. And there the wedding was held on 17 August, at St Peter and St Paul's Church, so that the local sailors and fishermen who had become their friends might also attend the ceremony.

John George Edward Davies, born at Leyton, Essex on 12 April, 1901,[20] was the only son of Henry Joseph Davies. The family had subsequently moved from Leyton to 36 Kingsway, Mortlake, Surrey, and John was still living there when he and Marjorie met. On 10 July, 1918, then aged 17, John had been indentured to the London

Wedding day, 17 August 1935.

shipping firm of George Thompson & Company for a three-year apprenticeship as a merchant seaman. It may have been from his father that John acquired his love of sailing and Henry stood surety for the indentures, which were returned to him by the company on 15 July, 1921, confirming that John had fulfilled his apprenticeship.[21]

How long John served in the merchant navy is not clear. At the outbreak of war in 1939 he was "in the rag-trade, in offices in St Paul's churchyard",[22] but he was also buying antiques. At the end of December 1940 he bought "an oak hall chest and an oak Welsh low chest", from The Antique Galleries in Sutton, Surrey, for £5 and £2.12.6d. Since he and Marjorie were then living in a rented flat on Richmond Hill the two chests may not have been for their own use and he was perhaps already repairing and selling antiques as a hobby.

Years later, following the war, "he joined his uncle's business",[23] possibly the London antiques showroom he was working for when he and Marjorie moved to Chailey in 1954. The Brighton antiques trade, he decided, was greatly inferior to London's and he would commute there daily, by car to Haywards Heath station and then by train. As a result, very little money remained from his earnings after expenses; and though he filled his spare time restoring furniture in his attic workshop at home he seems to have earned little from it.[24]

After their wedding reception at the Victory Hotel, they spent their honeymoon touring East Anglia in John's car, which Marjorie learnt to drive. From West Mersea they went on to Blakeney, Runton, King's Lynn, and Bradwell, photographing boats as often as each other. The following year they explored Itchenor, Bosham, Dell Quay and Emsworth – all popular sailing centres around Chichester Harbour – and finally Cowes.

The first boat they owned, according to Marjorie, was a nine-foot, single-sail dinghy, totally unsuited to either the Thames's currents under Tower Bridge, or the wide river mouth and the coast. Indeed, "on one trip from Twickenham boat yard down river to Mersea they encountered extremely rough weather near Maplin Sands and were lucky to reach the safety of the Essex harbour. Having been thoroughly ticked off by the Mersea fishermen for their daring, they bought a larger, 17-foot, boat with a cabin and got a tow from a tug boat to take it back up the river to Twickenham. Sadly, Marjorie recalled, it did not have an engine, so it could not be used to help the WWII Dunkirk rescue mission."[25]

Early holidays with John.

Marjorie and John were not well suited.

But apart from sailing, antiques and a love of dogs, Marjorie and John were not well matched. Years later she commented, "Poor John found life very difficult."[26] It was not for want of affection from his family. In Marjorie's words: "John's mother was a darling, and so were his two sisters, they all adored him."[27] It was as though he was trying to make people dislike him. He suffered violent mood swings and, if annoyed or upset, could remain silent for weeks, withdrawing totally from Marjorie and subjecting her to a tyranny of silence. Sometimes, according to one family member, he would strike her with his walking stick; and his habit of beating their dogs was thought to be excessive.[28] Yet he refused to accept that he might need professional help for what today might be considered bi-polar disorder.

It is possible that John's relative lack of income made him jealous of Marjorie's talent and the success of her work as an illustrator, which he never encouraged or praised.[29] It is noticeable that Marjorie's sketchbooks and records show no entries for the five years following her marriage, though she was still working full-time for Shand Kydd, and with the demands of housekeeping she may have had little spare time. She was also developing an interest in photography. One notebook reads: "Competition Entries: 'Daily Sketch' holiday snap, John in 'Mehalah', Sept. 1938 (returned Oct. 10, 38). Holiday Snaps comp. adv. sec. Eastbourne, 'Storm over Seven Sisters', Oct.20, 38."

John came from a generation that regarded it as a husband's duty to keep his wife in a style at least equal to that she had enjoyed in her father's house, and Alfred

Tea in the Tile House garden with brother Vic and Mab.

Clements was now very comfortably off. He had risen to company secretary of a large electrical firm, British Thompson Houston (BTH), makers of Mazda lamps, and had built an imposing new house with an acre of garden at Loudwater, Rickmansworth, known as The Tile House. Alfred's views on John are unknown, but Marjorie was well aware that John felt considerable antipathy to Alfred, certainly due to the deep affection he shared with his daughter, and possibly to his affluence. In her photos of a touring holiday with Mab and Alfred in May 1939, once more visiting Cornwall – and as usual photographing boats and boatmen – John does not appear.

With Mab (above) and her father, Marjorie toured the West Country in their chauffeur-driven car, 1939; (below) Marjorie, March 1941.

WAR AND THE WOMEN'S LAND ARMY, 1939–45

With the outbreak of World War II in September that year, Shand Kydd's factory was turned over to war work and Marjorie's design skills were no longer needed.

In the years since her marriage, she had suffered various forms of ill health and her doctor did not consider either her nerves or her body particularly strong. Nonetheless, ignoring his advice and in a kill-or-cure frame of mind,[30] she volunteered for the arduous work of the Women's Land Army (WLA), knowing it would be very much tougher than the gardening she'd loved as a child on her father's allotment. John also volunteered, hoping to serve in the navy, and while they both waited for their 'call up', Marjorie took a job handing out ration books in the local Food Office at Barnes, not far from their flat on Richmond Hill.

Marjorie would often vividly recount her visit to London in 1940 when John was on fire-watch duties, while waiting to be 'called up', at his offices by St Paul's Churchyard. "It turned out to be the worst night of the bombing raids on London. After the 'frantic clatter of incendiaries like hailstones the size of golf balls on the roofs all around John's office, the real bombing raid began.' Looking out, while John dealt with incendiaries nearby, she watched the fire wardens on St Paul's Cathedral kicking incendiary devices off the roof, and realised, 'ours was the only building not in flames'. Although quite frightened, she was awestruck at the Turner-like qualities that the light, flames and smoke created swirling around Wren's great dome."[31]

A small, black-and-white photo of her taken the following year shows her pensive, almost wistful, wearing a formal suit, her hair drawn plainly back in a bun. It may be an official portrait, taken for a wartime identity card, or her job in the food office. Or perhaps it just captures her wartime mood. For whatever reason, it has a melancholy air.

She was, however, now doing at least some drawing and painting again. A "Seaside Scene" done in November 1940 was given to her friend, Vi Johnson. Other pictures had a wartime theme: "Bunnies building", "Digging for Victory", "Bunnyland Air Raid". Early in 1942 she evidently painted a poster for Putney High School, one of the independent Girls' Public Day School Trust, not far from the flat.

On 25 February, the headmistress, Miss K. E. Chester, wrote to her from Upper Richmond Road: "Dear Mrs. Davies, We are all delighted with the most entertaining poster. It has been much admired by all the children going up and down stairs. I think some of them will envy your career! Perhaps you will come some day and tell us about your work."

It is most unlikely that Marjorie ever did, as the idea of public speaking would have terrified her. But she would have been glad to bring a little laughter into the lives of children still at school in wartime London – as she had been 20-odd years before. Most of the school's pupils had

Women's Land Army recruits gathered at Lewes, Sussex, May 1942: Marjorie (middle row, second left) and Mary Doherty (front row, first left) remained friends for life.

been evacuated to Caversham, Bath and Bristol, and the school building handed over to the Metropolitan Police. For the few girls remaining in London Miss Chester had found a house in Upper Richmond Road which could accommodate them, but not necessarily with suitable pictures and decorations. How Marjorie came to hear that a poster for them might be welcome is unknown, but it may have been through the Food Office.

At last, John was called up, to the army not the navy; and on 30 April, 1942 the county secretary of the local branch of the WLA, based in Guildford, wrote to Marjorie: "I am so glad to hear that you can accept the vacancy with the East Sussex War Agricultural Committee. You will be billeted for the first week at the Women's Land Army Hostel, Gracie Fields Orphanage, Peacehaven, near Brighton and at the end of this period you will be drafted into other billets in East Sussex…"[32] Enclosing a travel warrant, the secretary told her to report to the WLA area office in Lewes on 11 May, from where she would be transported to Peacehaven with other volunteers.

Having completed her week's induction, Marjorie's next billet turned out to be in Chailey, East Sussex. There she was detailed off to work on a farm between North Chailey and Newick; and to live with a group of girls in Cinder Paddocks, a detached house on Cinder Hill, Chailey, which had been requisitioned as a WLA hostel.

Now aged nearly 36, Marjorie was considerably older than most of the other WLA girls, many of whom were in their late teens or early twenties, and her maturity led her to become the leader, or 'Ganger', of the group at Cinder Paddocks.

The work was hard, the hours long, and at the end of each day it was her job to make up a log book of the hours every girl worked on each task, and keep the accounts. As usual, her record keeping was meticulous. Through the harsh winter of 1943–4 they were endlessly digging turnips, with just a brief respite sowing broad beans. On a December morning, from 8.30 through to 12.30, four girls could dig 70 buckets of turnips; and after an hour's break they would work another four hours, their hands numb with cold, till darkness closed in.

On Friday, Christmas Eve, they were still at it till nightfall and after only a three-day break they were back at work early on Tuesday morning. They worked all day New Year's Eve and must have been relieved to do a half-day on Saturday, 1 January. At Twelfth Night, 6 January,

(Above) Marjorie, right, kept a detailed log of their work; (below) Most of the girls were much younger.

they were still wrestling with the tedious turnips, but as spring advanced there were more interesting jobs. In April they were sorting and sacking old potatoes, planting new ones, cutting wood and making hurdles. The days' work now started at 7.45 a.m. and in a single morning, Marjorie and Florrie Ruddle could turn out a dozen hurdles on their own; so a week's tally for the two gangs amounted to 357 hurdles.

Hoeing, gathering weeds, cleaning the tool shed, tying pea-sticks, and stacking wood went on continuously through April to May, not to mention the unrecorded tasks of tractor driving, harnessing horses and carting heavy loads. Only rarely does Marjorie's log note, "1hr lost through rain". It must have been exceptionally wet on 10 May, for though "All reported at 8 o'clock", it was "Too wet – Rained all day" and no work was done. Later in May they were planting marrows and cucumbers, hoeing peas, and regularly "docking" and "swopping" – terms Marjorie would always use in future describing how to deal with invasive dock weeds and thistles.

At the end of what seems an exhausting week, the girls still found the energy to attend local dances and parties, though Marjorie rarely joined in. "She was older than us, and she was married," her friend Mary (later Mrs Mary Doherty) explained years later. "But she always sat

up until we got back to the hostel, to hear if we'd enjoyed ourselves, and what we'd been up to."[33]

Mary "thoroughly enjoyed the companionship of twenty other girls in the hostel," according to her sons; and "remained friends with most of the girls for the rest of her life. The work was extremely hard and arduous ... Not even a Doodle Bug crashing in the next field seemed to distract her from her adventures in the Land Army." In a poem Mary wrote about the Land Army, "she describes how she came to 'love the land' and how she felt she would never leave it ... the Land Army and the war were to shape [her] for the rest of her life."[34]

It was equally true of Marjorie, who remained always a passionate gardener and lover of wildlife. Among her stories of life in the WLA was being delayed one day by the work and rushing to Brighton to attend a piano recital. "It was a rare treat and the girls arrived only just in time. The usher directed her well forward, down the aisle to her seat, but to her dismay another patron had taken the seat. As Dame Myra Hess was by this time at the piano, Marjorie sank to the floor, whereupon her boots emitted a loud groaning squeak. Dame Myra immediately looked into the packed audience and eventually commenced the programme, leaving Marjorie feeling that all eyes were on her, and utterly spoiling her enjoyment of the concert."[35]

As the war drew to an end the hostel was due to close and the WLA team disband, yet VE Day – Victory in Europe in May 1945 – came and went, and the summer found Marjorie still living at the hostel and working for Mr Attrell, the owner of Warren Fruit Farm. But she was beginning to plan her post-war life.

Mary Doherty, who first met John during this period, remarked shortly before she died: "He was a rather strange man, I think. I'm not sure he entirely appreciated Marjorie."[36] How much Marjorie felt unappreciated by him, or whether either of them now wished to remain married, is not clear. On her birthday two years before, John had given her a copy of *The Dream of Fair Women*, by one of her favourite authors, Henry Williamson, and written in it: "Marjorie, With Best Wishes for June 5, 1943. May you have a Better and Happier Future, John." He was never effusive when inscribing books to her but this, written when she had been away twelve months in the Land Army, is longer, more thoughtful than usual. It has a rather final ring to it, as though they had reached the parting of their ways.

With the end of her war work in sight, Marjorie began

(Opposite) Many of the 'gang' remained life-long friends; (above) Marjorie in uniform, 1942–46.

seeking art commissions again, and it is noticeable that she was using her maiden name. In July she sent a drawing titled "The Dream of an Overworked Landgirl" to *Woman's Journal*, and signed herself Miss Marjorie Clements.

On 16 July the *Journal* replied (writing carelessly to her at Cinder Paddocks, Chatley, Essex – somehow it found its way to her): "We think this is delightful, but we are unable to make use of it in *Woman's Journal*. We have, therefore passed it on to another department in the hope that there may be an opening in the Children's papers. You will be hearing from them direct within a few days."

She did, four days later, but the editor of *Tiny Tots* and *Chicks' Own* returned the picture, saying: "The detail is interesting, but when reduced to half size a lot would be lost. It is a mistake to leave an empty space in the centre … The plate you did for *Tiny Tots Annual* in 1937 or 8 was better – "Dorothy's Dream" was the title. If you used a little more white it would brighten up your pictures. There is rather too much shadow and not enough sunlight. Contributions for annuals should be submitted in May and June."

Later that summer she sent the picture, with another, to Blackie and Son in London, again signing herself Miss Marjorie Clements. In her covering letter she explained that once released from the Land Army she would like to offer them more work. On 20 September they replied: "We have no immediate use for either of the drawings, but we would buy the Farm-Yard subject for possible future use. The price would be £5. If that is acceptable

(Opposite) "The Dream of an Overworked Landgirl", one of her favourite pictures, based on Wilding Farm, Chailey, 1945; (above) The WLA hostel "Cinder Paddocks" drawn as a 'doodle' for Mary Doherty, c. 1995.

please let us have an invoice. We shall be glad to hear from you when you are released."

The following year the hostel closed, Marjorie was released and John's war service ended. If either of them had had doubts about their marriage they put them aside. Marjorie carried on working as a farm hand and John came to share her accommodation at No. 5 Fruit Farm Cottages, which she rented from Mr Attrell for 3/- a week starting in September (1946).[37] But it was only a temporary arrangement, before they would both eventually return to "civvi street".

AFTER THE WAR

On 8 January, 1947 Marjorie wrote to Blackie and Son, signing herself – as always in future – Mrs Marjorie L. Davies. She wanted to know if they had yet reproduced her "Farm Yard" picture. It was one of her all-time favourites and she wanted to "borrow" it for an exhibition. On 22 January Blackie's replied that they had indeed published it, though they couldn't lay their hands on a proof; and would gladly lend her the original, so long as she agreed to return it. Hopefully they added: "If you have any line drawings of subjects suitable for children's books, we would be very glad to see them, and to make, if possible, a selection for reproduction." Five days later, having received her promise to return the original, they despatched it: "We enclose the drawing you would like

to exhibit and shall be glad if you will return it as soon as the exhibition is over… We trust the exhibition will be a success."

In view of Blackie's request to see other work, she sent nine line drawings on 25 February, and the company replied on 6 March: "We are retaining four of them – 'The Rabbits in the Timber Market', 'The Rabbits in the Snow Scene', 'The Owl Teaching' and 'The Birthday Party'". They offered £2.15 for each, and added: "If you care to submit a coloured picture on similar lines to the Birthday Party we think we could use it, but perhaps you had better let us see it in pencil form."

Within a fortnight she had sent them the pencil sketch, and when they replied three days later, with the money, they had already allocated the first three to their publication *The Cheery Book.* "The Birthday Party", they decided, "will make a good picture, but we would rather you squared up the subject, and if possible, introduce some feature into the gap at the bottom right-hand corner. The sketch should be finished in colour."

Soon she was producing more work at Blackie's request, and on 9 May (1947) they acknowledged receipt of "the finished drawing of the Rabbits' Picnic study and are glad to say that it has been carried out very satisfactorily, and the keeping down of the black line work to a minimum has been much to the advantage of the result."

With this amount of work building up, perhaps it was time to resume her career. She hadn't particularly enjoyed having Attrell as a boss, but working on the land, growing things, watching the Sussex wildlife, had become a joy, as deep and lasting as her love of painting.

Summer 1947 was her last at Warren's but not till the following May did Attrell write to her enclosing photos he had taken shortly before she left. They show her, the only woman among eight farm-hands, standing in dungarees and jumper, avoiding the camera and smiling instead at the Attrells' little daughter. Attrell apologised for the delay in sending them, explaining that he'd been too busy to get them developed, and he wasn't much of a letter-writer anyway.

By the time she received his letter, Marjorie and John had been living for some months with her father at The Tile House in Rickmansworth. Mab had died on 23 October, 1947 and at the end of that month Marjorie gave up her tenancy of the Fruit Farm Cottage. Maggie was still with Alfred as his housekeeper, but he was becoming increasingly frail and Marjorie was delighted to be close

(Opposite) Last days with the fruit farm workers in Chailey, autumn 1947; (above) Animal sketches filled pages of her notebook.

The Tile House, Rickmansworth, photographed in 1990.

to him during his declining years, despite the fact that John's attitude to him did not make it an easy situation for her.

Various members of the family later recalled visiting the house and being impressed by its size and its acre of beautiful garden, with a large stone-built summerhouse, rockeries and a croquet lawn, all looked after by Alfred's chauffeur-gardener.

In 2010, her niece Jacquie, Jack's eldest daughter, could remember it well: "The Tile House is still standing and in 2002 changed hands for a million pounds. I took Dad there some 20 odd years ago and the owners then were kind enough to show us around. It was built for my Grandfather and was such a lovely house; the chauffeur was called Bunker and Mrs Bunker used to help out in the house. He used to drive us around in a car that had a panel between the driver and passengers with a speaking tube through to him – but in those days we thought that everybody had one."

At the beginning of February, 1948, Marjorie responded to an advertisement placed in the personal columns of *The Times* and the *Daily Telegraph* by Kiddicraft Ltd, based in Barkston Gardens, Kensington, London. The company was inviting artists to send specimen designs for nursery friezes. It was exactly the sort of work she had enjoyed at Shand-Kydd. The response was huge and Marjorie was not successful. "Your style is extremely good and we think that it is quite possible that we may be able to give you some work later on," Kiddicraft replied on 16 February. "We have made a note of your name and address and may be able to get in touch with you later regarding book illustrations or something similar. It may be of interest to you to know that your pictures were among the nine best received out of 500."

From February to April her record book shows her making approaches to all her old contacts: at Pearson's, OUP, Warne's and Hutchinson's, and to Mr Penton, director of the Byron Studios, but with no success.

In March, Marjorie and John planned a holiday in their favourite region, East Anglia. But the White Lion Hotel at Blakeney hadn't any vacant rooms and they appear to have stayed at home, where Marjorie was keeping busy applying for membership of the local Watford and Bushey Art Society. It was an active group, with an annual summer exhibition and monthly sketching picnics. In June she was told that her application had been successful and she was appointed an Associate Member.

The following month she wrote once more to the White Lion. This time there was room, at £6 6s. each including dinner, and ration books would be needed. But Susan Long, the proprietress, warned them she couldn't provide food for the dogs, Marjorie and John's adored spaniels. She needed all her scraps for her hens.

At "Ricky", as the family called Rickmansworth, Marjorie was also trying to help her old Land Army friend Florrie Ruddle find a publisher. Florrie had written a series of Bird Poems and Dew Star Stories, which Marjorie forwarded for her to Blackie and Son. In April Blackie bought one of the poems with a line drawing, titled "Going to the Zoo". But in August they hastily returned some of Florrie's stories, explaining, "they are not up to our standard". If, however, Marjorie would "care to send us Miss Ruddle's stories and your own illustrations, we will go over them carefully." Marjorie recorded her expenses from the exercise, but no income.

Florrie was only one of the WLA girls who kept in regular touch with Marjorie. Elsie, Dolly, Jean and Mary all wrote, arranged visits and occasionally came to stay. In June they sent birthday greetings and in September planned a reunion in Brighton. But Marjorie didn't manage to join them. She was feeling despondent about not selling more drawings, and possibly about tensions at The Tile House. As she prepared a family tea party for Alfred's seventy-seventh birthday in October, she did not know she would soon begin one of the most productive and rewarding periods of her career.

Jill and Timmy, two of Marjorie and John's much-loved spaniels.

WORKING FOR ENID BLYTON, 1950–59

The story of how she came to work for Enid Blyton was one of Marjorie's favourites. When she wrote in January 1950, asking if she might send some specimen artwork, Enid was already well on the way to becoming the most prolific children's writer of the 20th century. The answer, as Marjorie told it, was a prompt and off-putting instruction not to send anything "unless it is really first-class".

In fact the reply, handwritten on 25 January from Enid's home, Green Hedges at Beaconsfield, was even more off-putting than Marjorie remembered. Discovered among Marjorie's papers, it read: "I am a very busy person, but if you like to send me a few of your drawings, both line and colour, I'll have a look at them. I hope you will not bother to send them unless you are pretty certain they are top-notch … It's a real plum to get an Enid Blyton book, as you know, and it's rare for a beginner to get a look in. Do not send enormous drawings, or a vast collection. I can tell at a glance from just a few whether your work is good and would suit me … Put in a stamped addressed return label with a sticky back, as all those details save my time. Send next week as I am a little less pressed for time then."[38]

Though Marjorie was by nature shy and modest in social situations, she was not unaware that her work was indeed "top-notch". She was not going to be put off and take umbrage at being treated as "a beginner". Nor was she going to be intimidated into waiting till next week

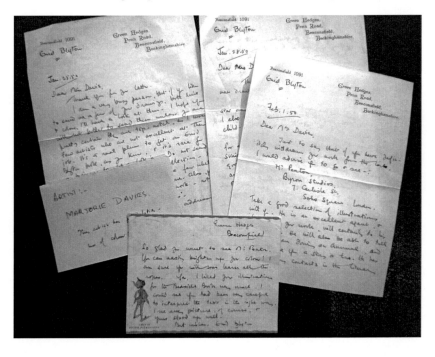

before sending her samples. Three days later, Enid had evidently received them and was writing again, this time more positively, yet still in the same domineering tone.

She liked them all, except the illustrations to Florrie Ruddle's "Dew Star" stories, which Blackie's had also turned down. "Some of your colour work is excellent," she wrote. "I also like your animals, and you have a good child-like sense of humour." She was now clearly anxious to secure Marjorie as one of her team of illustrators, and enclosed letters of introduction "to 2 or 3 of my publishers, with a view to getting you one or two of my stories for illustration in my own annuals ... I don't give introductions to many artists – only to about one in fifty – you will see that I really do consider you worth one!"

Not content with supplying the introductions, Enid continued with advice about using an agent, and how to approach the publishers. "Go and see them with your work if possible," she urged. Having signed the letter, she added a lengthy post-script suggesting Marjorie should offer to work initially as a "try-out" and should tell the publishers: "if they dislike your work ... they can reject it without payment. If you are certain of the standard of your work you can do this with the certainty 1) that it will make a good impression & 2) that it won't be rejected because it's too good for that!"

It is hard to imagine that "a busy person" would have spent so much time over a two-page letter if she had not been particularly keen for Marjorie to illustrate her work. And Enid's efforts did not stop there. On 1 February, she wrote yet again. Not knowing that Marjorie had, two years previously, approached Mr Penton of the Byron Studios with no success, Enid told her to visit him and gave his address.

"I [also] gave your name to one of my publishers the other day," Enid continued, "and there is a possibility, that if one of the regular artists fails to accept the commission of a story or two, they might write to you. Let me know what Mr. Penton says if you show him your work," she concluded.

Enid had done more than pass on Marjorie's name. The following day, Morrison & Gibb, the printers working on Enid's *Second Bedside Book* for her publisher, Arthur Barker, wrote: "Miss Blyton has requested us to send instructions for the production of line drawings. We are enclosing article Michael's Tail for which we require 10 illustrations in 2 colour line, and we should be grateful if you could produce these in black drawings, completing

THE BEAR BEGAN TO CRY.

HE SWUNG HIS NEW TAIL.

Marjorie's first pictures for Enid, "Michael's Tail", appeared in the Second Bedside Book, *August 1950.*

" DON'T CRY," SHE SAID.

Initial sketches for "How Silly", Sunny Stories, *August 1951.*

the second colour on transparent paper to save redrawing for blockmaking."

By 16 February Marjorie had despatched the pictures to the printers' works at Tanfield in Edinburgh; and in less than a fortnight she had completed three more commissions for the book: "A Mix-Up", "Is Your Name Here?", and "Riddle-Me-Ree". Acknowledging them, the printers added: "These appear to be very satisfactory, but we are sending them on to Miss Blyton for her approval."

It was standard practice for Enid to personally vet illustrations. As an exhibition of Marjorie's work, staged at Ditchling Museum in 2000, pointed out: "Blyton chose her artists with great care and personally approved all the artwork for her magazines and books. For nearly 10 years Marjorie was part of a small team of classic illustrators who did much to make Enid the most commercially successful children's author of the day."

Clearly Miss Blyton had approved very much of Marjorie's pictures for her *Second Bedside Book*, which appeared that summer,[39] and now the work began pouring in. On 2 March, Newnes & Pearson's, publishers of Enid's highly popular children's magazine, *Sunny Stories*, invited Marjorie to "bring some of your drawings here next Wednesday"; and on 7 June the first of her pictures appeared in the magazine – two line drawings for "A Letter from our Little Mouse".

Meanwhile, Marjorie had followed up Enid's instruction to contact Mr Penton of the Byron Studios, at 7 Carlisle Street, Soho Square. His earlier discouraging response, noted in Marjorie's records, is confirmed by Enid's daughter, Imogen Smallwood. She was told by Marjorie that he had initially been critical of her use of colour.[40] Enid obviously thought otherwise, for on a scrap of paper Enid had scribbled, "ARTIST – MARJORIE DAVIES. This artist has possibilities – use of colour good." It was possibly intended as a recommendation to one of her publishers and how it ended up in Marjorie's papers is unknown.

Since writing that, Enid must have been made aware of Mr Penton's reservations, for on an undated card, sent from Green Hedges, she wrote to Marjorie: "So glad you went to see Mr Penton. You can easily brighten up your colour: I am sure you will soon learn all the ropes. Yes, I liked your illustrations for the *Bedside Book* very much. I could see you had been very careful to interpret the text in the right way. I see every picture, of course, and yours stood up well. Best wishes, Enid Blyton."

With Enid's approval, Mr Penton had little choice but to commission Marjorie to work on the next book he was handling for her, *The Buttercup Story Book*, another volume of children's stories, poems and puzzles. When it was published in April the following year it contained seven different items illustrated by Marjorie. Each one had up to seven pictures and earned her in total £47.11.6d, "less £9.10.4d commission to the Byron Studios".

Over the next decade, commissioned through Enid's numerous different publishers, printers and agents, Marjorie produced literally hundreds of pictures and line-drawings for her weekly and fortnightly magazines, annuals and storybooks.[41]

For the *Third Bedside Book*, for example (published August 1951) Marjorie illustrated three major stories "When Michael Missed the Bus", "The Angry Wasp" and "The Mischievous Panda", each needing four or more

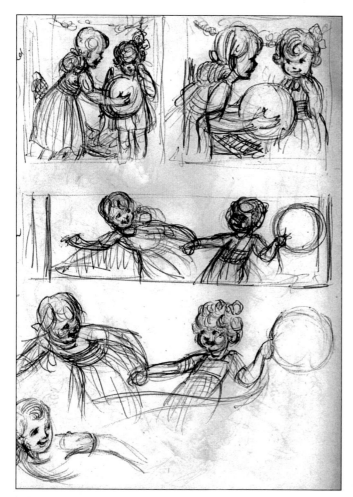

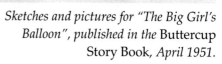

Sketches and pictures for "The Big Girl's Balloon", published in the Buttercup Story Book, *April 1951.*

HIS FATHER LOOKED UP FROM HIS PAPER.

MICHAEL MISSED THE BUS!

MICHAEL REACHED OUT AND TOOK HOLD.

"When Michael Missed the Bus" was one of five features Marjorie illustrated for Enid's Third Bedside Book, *August 1951.*

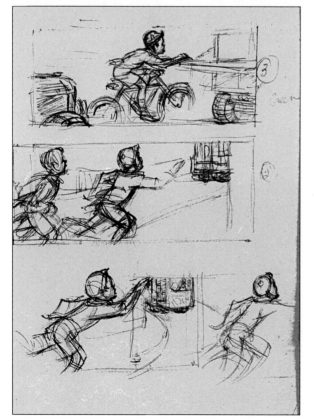

THE ANGRY WASP

SHE SNATCHED AT JOAN'S HAIR-RIBBON.

THE WASP BECAME ANGRY.

HER MOTHER WAS DELIGHTED.

pictures; plus two single-page items, "Hidden Flowers" and "A Funny Little Puzzle". For the ninth in the series (July 1957) she drew the pictures for six different items; the title, half-title and contents pages; and "a superb dust-wrapper".[42]

Only one of Marjorie's commissions for Enid was not a success. In December 1951 she was asked to illustrate a Noddy story, "Run, Noddy, Run", and "A letter from Little Noddy", for *Sunny Stories*. It was a rare appearance for Noddy in the magazine, as he was normally the subject of his own books; and Marjorie had not appreciated that Noddy's original, Dutch, illustrator had created an image so popular that it had to be copied exactly. Her own efforts were returned and, as she recorded, "All redrawn to previous character". Her sketchbook reveals the transformation from her own idea of Noddy to the standardised version. Talking about her Noddy efforts years later, she remarked, "I was never asked again."[43]

"The Angry Wasp" (opposite) and "The Mischievous Panda" (above) also appeared in the Third Bedside Book.

A Letter from LITTLE NODDY.

Hallo, Children!

I'm nodding my head at you. Can you see me? It goes nodding up and down all the time, even when I want to say "No."

I wish I could take you for a ride in my little car. If ever you come to Toyland, where I live, will you please let me drive you round to see the sights? I can take you to Humming Top Town, or Bouncing Ball Village, or to see all the animals in the Noah's Ark. And, of course, I'll be sure to take you to tea with Big-Ears, my friend, who lives in a toadstool house.

Some cheerful nod-nod-nods from

LITTLE NODDY.

Marjorie's original Noddy sketches had to be reworked before he was published in his usual style in Sunny Stories, *February 1952.*

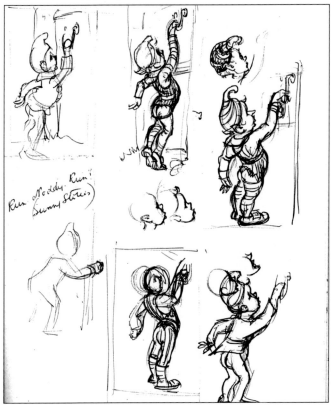

UP HE WENT, BRANCH BY BRANCH.

"Billy-up-the-Tree" (above and left) and "One Snowy Night" (below and opposite) were both commissioned for the Fourth Bedside Book, *June 1952.*

THEY STOOD THERE IN A RING.

For the Water-Lily Story Book, *June 1953, Marjorie illustrated "Poor Little Bear" (yet another story of a toy without a tail), "When Sheila Ran Away" and five other features, earning £43.14s 'less £8.14.9d commission' to Mr Penton.*

That experience may have shaken her confidence a little. In January 1952, she wrote to Morrison & Gibb, asking them to send her printed specimens of the illustrations she had done, almost certainly with a view to sending them to other publishers to build up new outlets, in case her work for Miss Blyton should come to an end.

She approached at least one other company, Lutterworth Periodicals, whose titles included the *Boy's Own Paper*, *Heiress* and *Playways*, and in September (1952) wrote to the art editor offering to send specimens of her work. He replied the following day: "If you will do so I shall be pleased to see them, and will return them to you promptly." After she forwarded him a number of drawings he returned them, having given them "careful examination". There was nothing he could ask her to do at the moment, but he promised to add her name to their register of artists.

Despite the huge quantity of work she was producing, there was still time for occasional holidays. With John she spent Easter 1950 in Mersea again and went on to Norwich, where John recorded, in a copy of *Marshland Adventure* by J. Wentworth Day, one of his favourite authors: "Good Inn – Maid's head. Antiques – Townshead, Elm Street, Norwich. Major Mace Antiques, Prince of Wales Road, Norwich. Mr Hyles, Bridge Inn, Acle, N'folk." In 1951 they toured the West Country, visiting Lyme Regis, Sidmouth and Minehead, and John gave her a copy of *My Cousin Rachel* by West Country author Daphne du Maurier.

Marjorie need not have worried that her work might dry up. Enid did leave *Sunny Stories*, but its new editors would continue to commission her until September 1953. And Enid was about to launch a new children's journal that would need hundreds more of Marjorie's illustrations. On 10 February, 1953, Audrey White of Evans Brothers wrote from their offices in Russell Square: "Dear Mrs Davies, Miss Enid Blyton is going to write a complete magazine for children, to be known as ENID BLYTON'S MAGAZINE, which we are to publish for her. We hope to publish the first issue on March 18th and Miss Blyton has suggested that we ask you to illustrate stories for the magazine from time to time. I therefore enclose the typescript of GOBBLE-GOBBLE-GOBBLE! together with a rough layout giving the space of illustrations. I have shaded the area available on each page. The drawings, which should be as bold as possible, are to be in line – black only on some pages and black and red where

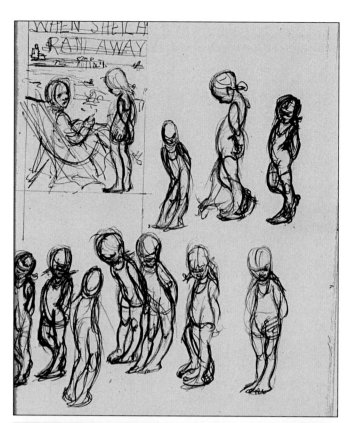

Marjorie's first cover-story for Enid Blyton's Magazine *was "The Ship in the Bottle", March 1953 (top); followed by "Peculiar Happenings", January 1954.*

marked. Line tints can be used, but I think we should not make use of these on faces."

If Marjorie wanted to do the title lettering, too, that would be fine, Audrey White went on, but most important was the deadline. The drawings would be needed "by March 9th at the latest". Marjorie wrote by return, accepting the commission and suggesting that she should "add the second colour on Kodatrace". Soon Audrey White wrote again, thanking her "for the truly delightful drawings for THE SHIP IN THE BOTTLE I really am most pleased with these." So pleased, in fact, that Marjorie's pictures formed the cover and main story for the May issue.

At the same time as supplying work for the magazines, Marjorie was still in demand for the 'flower books'. Mr Penton confirmed on 7 September (1953) that he had received her pictures for seven different features in *The Marigold Story Book*, and added: "All the drawings seem to me to be delightful, as usual."

Audrey White, too, was treating Marjorie as a trusted member of the team. Sending instructions to The Tile House in December, she wrote: "Enclosed are our formal agreements for PECULIAR HAPPENINGS. Would you please sign and return the appropriate form in the usual way." Again Marjorie's illustrations for "Peculiar Happenings" were used as the cover picture and lead story in the January 1954 issue and she received nine guineas – around £600 in today's money.

Although Marjorie and John were still living at The Tile House, and remained there until at least May 1954, Alfred had died in 1953. It was her share of his estate, Marjorie said,[44] that enabled them to buy a home of their own. In February 1948, after Mab's death, Alfred had made a new will leaving the bulk of his estate equally between his four children. There was however, an additional clause, pointing out that Marjorie had already received, "some years prior to the date of this will", investments then valued at £1,400, which were to be taken into account when dividing the estate. Those investments, in what was then Beecham's pharmaceutical company, later Smith Kline Beecham, would provide her with a useful income for the rest of her life.

Apart from his gold watch, marble clock and some jewellery, which went to Jack, Alfred bequeathed to his daughter "all my household furniture plate plated articles linen glass china books". It was virtually the entire contents of The Tile House, far more than she and

John would need to furnish their own home. It is perhaps not surprising that the contents went to Marjorie, since Jack had already established his own home. So had Con, who went on to a long and steady career with a major insurance company. Vic, however, was less successful. His business ventures did not turn out well and in the 1970s he and his wife Anne were living in a mobile home – "somewhere in Bracknell, which to the Clements family made him a bit of an exile."[45]

RETURN TO CHAILEY, 1954

With The Tile House up for sale, Marjorie and John "had to rush" to find a new home, and though they went house-hunting around their favourite haunts in Essex, it was in Chailey that they found the property they wanted. "It had to be an old cottage," Marjorie said, still living in it 50 years later. The estate agents had advertised "Ades Cottage", also known as Number 2 Coppard's Bridge Cottages, as "A charming little old-world cottage … offered at the very modest price of £2,000, freehold." It was barely 300 yards from Cinder Paddocks, yet, "I hadn't even remembered it," Marjorie said. "It was hidden behind a large hedge."[46]

She phoned the estate agents early in January (1954) only to learn that it had already been "sold within 48 hours of the first applicant who inspected". The purchase, however, had not gone through and it was now back on the market. On 16 February Marjorie wrote arranging to collect the key from Mr Spicer, who lived in the adjoining cottage, Number 1, with his daughter and her husband, Dorothy and Charlie Thorne. [47]

The three-bedroom property was part of a timber-framed, 15th century hall house that had been divided into two cottages early in the 19th century. Originally it had been thatched, but a fire, probably in the 18th century, had burnt the thatch and it had been replaced with tiles. At some time the ground-floor wattle-and-daub walls had been replaced by bricks, and tile-hanging had been added to the front of the house. Only in the rear wall and interior were its massive oak beams exposed, hinting at the house's origins. Its real antiquity was not revealed until years after John's death but it was clearly old and attractive, and it was surrounded by familiar fields and woods where they could walk the dogs.

But it needed plenty of work done on it. The surveyors' report, sent to Marjorie on 5 March, "does not make very good reading", the firm admitted.[48] The roof needed

(Top) No. 2 Coppard's Bridge, renamed "Timestone Cottage" by Marjorie and John; (above) The adjoining cottage, No. 1, both drawn in the 1990s.

attention, the house was damp, the "plaster work to the majority of the rooms is bulged and away from its key". The drainage was inadequate and in general "its maintenance has been sadly neglected". Confirming that verdict, a Newick building company reported a few days later: "The roof is in a very bad state of repair ... There is no damp proof course ...Most timbers are affected by worm or disease ... The ceiling over the small fireplace is sagging, and the whole centre panel will have to come down ..."[49]

None of that put them off. They loved it and on 7 May they bought it. But it was another local builder, Beard's,[50] who got the repair job and in September invoiced them for "88 Old Paving bricks" and for "Taking off tiles, felting, rebattening and relaying tiles, replacing gutter ... and making good joints". They made a bonfire in the garden of all the wooden pegs that had held the tiles in place, Marjorie recalled.[51]

Perhaps most importantly, Beard's upgraded the bathroom, replacing the "Separate chemical closet" with a modern WC inside the bathroom, and an outside WC in one of the two small outhouses at the back of the building. Again in September they invoiced for: "Excavating and building septic tank and necessary drainage for 2 WCs, 3 gulleys for such and bath wastes, Supplying 2 high level WC suites with single plastic seats and running water supply to same as per estimate sent to Mr Humphries [the previous owner] December 10, 1953 – £139.12.6d." There was an extra £9.12.7d for the "rise of wages and materials"; and £2.0.11d" for "one low level WC suite and double flap seat": which replaced the original plan for a high-level suite in the bathroom, doubtless due to the low level of the ceiling.

At the end of the following year, December 31, 1955, Beard's invoiced them for work to the "Sitting Room Fire Place"; and for "Building new garage, taking down old, excavating ..." a total of £230.14.3d. Removing the "sagging" ceiling was not part of the work: "We decided to leave it and it's never come down," she said. [52]

The sitting room had a huge inglenook fireplace and the kitchen a large leaded-light window from which Marjorie could survey the whole rear garden. The attic became a workshop where John repaired and stored bits of antique furniture. The rear garden was soon transformed from a kitchen garden into a picturesque place with level lawns, herbaceous borders, pathways and brick walls, all carefully planted with trees and

(Opposite above): "Timestone Cottage" from the rear garden; and (below) from the front of No. 1 Coppard's Bridge, seen in the foreground; watercolours, 1976.

Two of Marjorie's eleven cover-story illustrations for Enid's magazine: "Well, of all the Peculiar Things", April 1958 (top) and "What a Piece of Luck", July 1958.

shrubs chosen with an artist's eye for colour and leaf-shape.

One of the small bedrooms, tucked under a sloping roof, became known as Marjorie's studio[53] and for the next five years she continued regularly despatching illustrations to both Morrison & Gibb for Enid Blyton's books, and to Evans Bros. for *Enid Blyton's Magazine*.

The years working for Blyton were, she said, the happiest times of her professional life.[54] She often laughingly recalled her worst commercial decision as her refusal to take over illustrating one of Enid's main story-book series. Blyton's annuals and magazines always contained illustrations by several different artists, but for her series Enid liked to use only one of her favourites, so that the images remained consistent. Eileen Soper always illustrated *The Famous Five*, Harmsen van der Beek did *Noddy* (until his sudden death) and for the first four *Secret Seven* books, Enid chose George Brook. But in 1952 she was considering a different artist for *The Secret Seven*, and it seems most likely that those were the characters she offered Marjorie, though Marjorie's later recollections implied it was *The Famous Five*.[55]

Despite the move to Chailey and her work on the garden, through 1956 and 1957 Marjorie continued producing pictures for almost every issue of Blyton's magazine. But in 1958 she was again looking for other outlets for her work. Still with the help of the Link Studios, she was trying to illustrate schoolgirls' magazines, though she was far from certain she could get the figures right.

On 21 November, Elizabeth White wrote to her from the Link: "I am sure that as soon as you become confident you'll manage the school girls quite well. They need just a little more drawing on the faces – the features must be drawn in more detail and they are just a little too young for the A.P. convention of a school girl, who has a pretty face of a girl of 18–20, on a slim figure of almost adult proportions. You're getting very near what they want, so stop jittering."

The studio was also attempting to get her commissions with other companies who published children's painting books and stories, but again with mixed success. Explaining the changes that Dean and Sons' editor was asking for, Elizabeth wrote: "I'm sorry I have to return the Dean's sketches, but please don't be discouraged …This sounds an awful lot [of changes], but I think it is fairly straightforward … However, she [the editor] does like your work, and I am enclosing MSS for a children's story,

'Tony's Tortoise', of the 7–9 age group, with which you will be more at home. I am only sorry you did not come along earlier, before all these children's stories were given out. A very strong open line is required, with solid blacks and no hatching. It must be even stronger than the school-girls illus. because larger type is used."

Spring 1959 saw Marjorie still struggling to find the right form. On 20 April, Elizabeth thanked her for some sketches, adding:"I have taken them along to the publishers but I'm afraid they are not quite what they want yet. I think you can do it though so I am sending you now two examples of the kind of thing. You will see that they are much brighter in colour. Although the editor likes your pages of bunnies he really wants something bolder and cleaner as in this cover by Kennedy. There is quite a good opening here so it is worth having a really good go."[56]

In March she sent The Link some colour plates for: "Pixie Market", "Snow Fairies", "Pixie Playground" and "Digging for Victory (Rabbits)", but they were returned in July. Her sketchbook for April shows roughs for a story called "Snake in the Grass" by Naunton Lane (for Birn Bros), but no further published pictures, except for Enid.

The illustrations she had done for *the Eleventh Bedside Book*, five different features and the end-papers, appeared in July 1959. And for the last two issues of *Enid Blyton's Magazine*, which closed in September 1959, she had produced the covers and pictures for a two-part main story about "A Dog Named Timmy". The pictures, however, were not based on Marjorie's own adored black spaniel, also named Timmy.

For the final two issues of Enid Blyton's Magazine, *which ceased publication in September 1959, Marjorie illustrated the two-part cover-story "A Dog Called Timmy".*

Due to a paper strike, the final issue was delayed from June. On 6 September, three days before it went on sale, Enid wrote to Marjorie, as usual from her home, Green Hedges in Beaconsfield. She had written the previous December to thank Marjorie for a donation to the Home that she had founded for thirty children. Now she wrote a long three-page letter, thanking her for another donation, but also for all her work, and explaining why she had decided to end the magazine:

"Dear Mrs Davies,
What a wonderful surprise you gave me – and how very very generous of you! I was quite overcome when I saw the cheque and read your letter. Thank you more than I can say – for both. I am sad too that you and I will not be working together on my magazine any more … I feel it would be selfish to go on, now that my husband has retired … the magazine is the one thing that ties me down and which has to go with me wherever I go (the work I mean!) … And now I must thank you for all your good (& most dependable work) and say that I hope this won't be the end of all collaboration!
All the best to you, Yours very sincerely,
Enid Blyton."

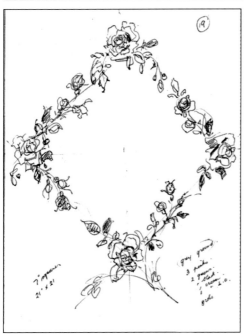

But it *was* the end of their collaboration; and for Marjorie it was the end of an era. She had admired Enid's professionalism and her charity work, and though she recognised that Enid was demanding, she never found her difficult, and thoroughly enjoyed illustrating her stories.

LIFE IN CHAILEY, 1959–67

The following month Marjorie, now aged 53, wrote to Newnes, publishers of *Sunny Stories*, hoping they might have work for her again. She had done nothing for them for six years and now, they responded: "You will appreciate, of course, that we have a regular team of artists working for us at the present time." She fared no better with Sampson Low, who replied: "There is nothing I could ask you to undertake for the present time." Nor with Collins, because: "the bulk of our illustration work for next year's programme has already been commissioned." They'd keep her name on file, but she noted in her record book that she was "not very hopeful". She tried Mr Phillips at Lutterworth's again, but recorded sadly: "Mr Phillips gone. Lutterworth's now do no children's work."

For their summer holiday that July Marjorie and John went to Clevedon, and the following summer Purbeck. Wherever they went they would look in at antiques showrooms and auctions, as they did throughout the year in Sussex, making day trips to Rye, Lewes and country-house sales.

At home there were the dogs to walk, the garden to tend and the housekeeping to occupy her, but it was not enough, and after some months without commissions she decided to see if she could revive the design skills she had developed at Shand Kydd. Early in January 1961 she paid for a course in textile, carpet and wallpaper design with The Textile Studio, based in Harrow. The idea was that students should use the studio's tuition and textbook to create designs and submit them for criticism; and if good enough the studio would retain them for possible sale to clients. Her first two efforts were returned, but at least the next four were "retained to show to the trade".

In early summer, having completed 11 designs, she was beginning to doubt her success with the lessons, for on 14 June the principal, David West, wrote to her: "Your question as to your future prospects and whether or not it is worth your while to take further lessons, is a very natural one, in view of the fact that I have retained so

(Above) Dorothy and Charlie Thorne, left and right, were already living at No. 1 Coppard's Bridge when Marjorie and John moved in next door in 1954.

(Right, above and below) After years working for Enid, tending the garden and walking the dogs with John were not enough to occupy her.

(Opposite, top) "A Dog Called Timmy" proved the end of Marjorie's long and happy collaboration with Enid;

(opposite below) "Rose Trellis" wall-paper design, March 1963.

John was rarely seen without his pipe.

many of your designs, out of which one has been sold." Discussing her latest submission he summed up: "delightful drawing and painting, which is a pleasure to see, but in colouring technique, etc, it has important defects."

Nonetheless, he hoped she would continue; and she did, off and on until 1967, creating some thirty designs, often large and elaborately worked up in colour, for carpets and wallpapers. Only three ever found buyers, and one was entered unsuccessfully for a competition.

In 1963 she sent some of her wallpaper designs to her old boss at Shand Kydd, Mr Roland, wondering if he might be interested. Her letter is typical of her diffidence: "Living in rather a remote spot, and having little opportunity for studying current trends, I fear I may be rather out of touch." She didn't keep his reply, but she noted: "March 24. No luck but contact Donald Melbourne and go up during week commencing June 24."

If she went, she didn't keep a record, and it led to nothing. She would have disliked the idea of meeting someone new and 'selling herself'. The steady deterioration in her hearing, coupled with her shyness, made her uncertain with strangers, and she was not fond of formal occasions or large social gatherings. She had had surgery on the stapes in both her ears before 1939 and a bomb-blast the night she was at St Paul's meant she "lost the hearing in my right ear completely".[57] Even with an aid she had great difficulty hearing, or knowing from which direction sounds came.

Then in 1967, on 1 December, after a brief illness, John died in Bevendean Hospital, Brighton. He had been a heavy pipe smoker for years and his lung cancer, though unsurprising, was not detected until it was beyond treatment. Their doctor, Marjorie recalled, quietly told her it was pointless for her to continue to try and persuade him to give up his pipe; and since it gave him some pleasure she abandoned her efforts. [58]

He had not been an easy person to live with – at times deliberately unkind – and he had found it hard to cope with the loss of his job in London, probably early in 1967.[59] At home all day, his moods could only have impinged on Marjorie more heavily. After she died, two small crates of wine glasses were found in her studio, still wrapped in newspaper from 1954 and never opened since she brought them from The Tile House. John had disliked anything to do with her father and perhaps that went for the glasses, too.

WIDOWHOOD AND WATERCOLOURS, 1967–1985

Living alone in a country cottage might have seemed a daunting prospect to many, but Marjorie was both good at making friends and spending time on her own. She seems never to have doubted that she wanted to stay put, despite selling John's car and giving up driving. She had an amiable neighbour in Dorothy Thorne and they had much in common. Dorothy had been a widow for five years;[60] she, too, did not have children; and she was an

Sketchbook watercolour, "Falmer, 1978"

equally keen gardener, though more interested in fruit and vegetables than flowers. There was a bus service from 'The Point' at the end of the lane, half a mile away, to the post office, or six miles further into Lewes. And Chailey parish, though lacking a real centre, had a branch of the Women's Institute to which she, Dorothy and another friend, Amy Jennings, all belonged. Besides, Marjorie had her painting to return to.

In July 1970 she enrolled for a postal art course with the Famous Artists School, an American organisation with offices in Amsterdam, where the tutors were based, and an administration address in London.

The course involved twenty assignments, each of which came with detailed instructions on how to approach the different subject, starting with three studies in oils. Each time her work was returned with a detailed critique and a grade: Bs and B+ for the three oils. The next two assignments were watercolours. "What makes your little painting so effective is the simplicity of the washes," the tutor replied, giving her an A for assignment four.

"New Gate, Winchelsea, 1988", one of many watercolours accepted for the Society of Women Artists' annual London exhibition.

Assignment five earned her an A– and "Congratulations on your fine handling of the watercolour medium"; though there was also a hint that she should add some warm colour and soften the edges of each shape.

Her still-life pencil sketch, life drawings and portraits were deemed "Excellent" and returning her exercise in illustration the tutor commented: "I cannot improve your sketches." Coming after ten years without encouragement to do any serious painting, and evidently without any commissions, it must have been a tremendous boost to her confidence.

The textiles design course had led to no work and little pleasure. Watercolour painting and landscapes were a different matter. By 1972 she had taken them up seriously and soon became an award-winning landscape painter, successfully submitting work to national competitions, such as the 1973 *Sunday People*'s National Housewives' Painting Competition. Her entry, a watercolour titled "Against the Sun" was selected by the three judges, including Sir John Rothenstein, former director of the Tate, for display at the Royal Festival Hall, where she was invited to a special awards ceremony on 5 September. She did not gain a top prize, but she did obtain the judges' autographs.

Through the 1970s and 80s her work was also accepted for the annual London exhibitions staged by the Society of Women Artists. She frequently had three or four pictures accepted and hung, but she never sought membership of the SWA by submitting the necessary five or six subjects they required. And sadly the SWA did not relax its rules, even though she was 83 when they accepted four of her pictures, "Upstairs, Downstairs", "The Old Dee Bridge", "New Gate, Winchelsea", and "Massa Lubrense, nr Sorrento", to hang in their 1989 exhibition at Westminster Central Hall.

Many of the paintings Marjorie submitted for exhibition were the result of painting trips she undertook with Galleon Holidays. Galleon was the leading operator in the field, offering high-quality trips for high-quality artists. Yet despite such talented competitors, in 1980 Marjorie won Galleon's coveted medal, the Wattie Award, for the best painting of the year, presented to her in Chichester on 15 August.

There is no evidence that with John she ever went abroad, but with Galleon she travelled widely, thoroughly enjoying the chance to paint in interesting locations: Italy, twice to Spain – Palamos in 1973 and Mojacar the following

Detail from "Timestone Garden",
1960s sketchbook.

Finished watercolours painted in Spain, c. 1973.

*Sketchbooks watercolours: untitled (left)
and Makarska, Yugoslavia, 1978 (below).*

This page: Finished watercolour of Chichester Harbour, Sussex, c. 1978 and watercolour sketch of Vixengrove Farm, Chailey, 1976.

Facing page: Watercolour sketches of Southease Church and village, Sussex, 1977.

Pen-and-ink drawings for Chailey News:
1976 (top) and St Peter's School, c. 2000.

year; Greece, France, Austria; Rhodes in 1983, and Yugoslavia – a particular favourite, which she first visited in September 1976, flying from Gatwick to Dubrovnik and staying at the Hotel Park on the island of Korcula.

Her tutors on these holiday courses, all experts, included the well-known artist Edward Wesson, her favourite modern UK watercolourist; and John Seabrook, another water-colour specialist, who greatly admired Marjorie's work.[61] Some of her fellow travellers, as dedicated and gifted as she was, became firm friends and joined her on subsequent holidays, sometimes several in a year. They also visited her in Chailey, as did her family, particularly her brother Jack and his wife Edna and their daughters, Jacquie, Gill and Angie; and in 1975, for the first time from Australia, Davydd Shaw.

In 1976, as she approached her 70th birthday, her days were filled with a constant round of gardening, painting, letters, phone calls and visits to and from friends and family. In January she was planning a fortnight in Italy with Galleon, and a spring trip to the Isle of Wight to stay with Jack and Edna and see her nieces. Back in Chailey rarely a day passed without a visit from friends and neighbours; tea or lunch with Dorothy; and periodic trips to Brighton and Haywards Heath usually by bus from 'The Point'. Weekly shopping meant a visit to the village stores and post office at Setfords in South Chailey, either walking the three-mile round trip or, on rare occasions, driven by "Eddie", the Rev. Edwin Matthias, rector of St Peter's parish church. Marjorie sometimes attended church with Dorothy and Amy and took communion, but she was not a regular member of the rector's flock.

Eddie wasn't too fussy about that, and he was a fan of her painting. He not only encouraged her to enter his painting exhibitions at the church, he persuaded her to produce pen-and-ink drawings for the covers of his monthly parish newsletter. At first it was not an exclusive job, and her earliest covers (1975/6) were usually of children: gathering vegetables for harvest festival, watching a crib for Christmas, and so on. Later she became the sole illustrator and the subjects were always local scenes and buildings, for which she would carefully pencil in the perspective lines using her old T-square. Even if she had to "cook the picture", her words, by pushing a tree or a garage to a slightly different position to create a more pleasing structure, it was important to her that the perspectives were perfectly aligned.

By the late 1970s so many Chailey pensioners needed transport to the village shop that Eddie toured the parish in the church mini-bus once a week collecting them from their houses. But not until Marjorie was well into her 80s would she agree to be collected from her door. She insisted she liked the walk to the end of the lane, but privately admitted she was petrified by Eddie's driving, which she put down to him being in the air force during the war.[62]

From the mid-1980s Marjorie was beginning to limit her travels. In 1983 she went to Usk in Gwent, still with Galleon; the following year she was painting in West Sussex, near Boxgrove Priory. In 1986 she was abroad again, at Bruges. But after that it was Earnley Concourse near Chichester (1988); Juniper Hall in Surrey; another Galleon holiday at Plumpton College, tutored for the last time by John Seabrook; and finally in 1990, a return visit to The Old Rectory adult education centre at Fittleworth, West Sussex.

At home she enjoyed regular days out with local friends, like Monica Hecks, painting neighbouring villages, the South Downs, and the Ouse Valley churches. Her easel, paintbox and camping stool were kept permanently in the corner of the dining room. But as such trips became more difficult, she took to painting fewer landscapes and more children's pictures. From her seat at the window of her kitchen, she never tired of watching the changing seasons and the wildlife in her garden, which contained a souvenir of one of her foreign holidays: a conifer tree grown from seed she had collected in Salvador Dali's garden near Cadaques during a painting holiday in Spain.

(Top) Watercolour study "Malling Church with Monica, 1989"; (above) Marjorie in Bruges, 1986; (left) Watercolour sketch, untitled.

"DOODLING" AT HOME

Her chief delight now became "doodling", as she called it. Sometimes she would turn the view from her window into an imaginary world of small animals and gnomes. At other times it took only a single bunch of flowers to inspire her. The result would be an intricate scene of rabbits, mice or elves, gathering primroses and catkins for their shop, playing around the sundial, picking daisies, having a bonfire; or an entire imaginary village scene.

Just as the adventures of Rosebud and Willow, Timothy and Titus, Lopear and Bobtail, had streamed from her drawing board half a century earlier, so now from the same board – balanced for at least an hour every morning in the kitchen window – there came a procession of enchanting furry creatures and fairies, frequently up to no good, and drawn with the same old humour and inventiveness.

It was a delight to her and a joy to her family and friends, who besieged her with commissions for what, despite their appreciation, she persisted in calling "doodles". Most were done for friends, but a few were done for herself and reproduced as her own Christmas

Watercolour "doodles"1985–2000 – each one included, somewhere, her trademark ladybird.

(Right) Detail from "Easter Doodle", c. 1988; (below) "Village Scene" was drawn for herself, c. 1993;

(Opposite, above) "The Market Square" became a greetings card, c. 1999; (below) "Bedtime Story", 1985.

*(Above) "The Royal Oak,
Newick", 1995, began as a
pen-and-ink drawing
(facing page) for the parish
magazine; (right) Christmas
card 2005; (below) Marjorie
at home, 1999.*

cards and notelets. Her niece Jacquie turned others into greetings cards, and Eddie Matthias prompted her to produce a picture for every month of the year to illustrate a children's calendar (later published by his daughter).

In 1995 she again submitted five pictures for the local art exhibition in St Peter's; and the following year she was asked to design a new village sign for Chailey, which was fabricated in metal and erected on the village green in front of the parish church.

As well as continuing with watercolours, in her 80s Marjorie produced a series of ceramics, the subjects always being small animals – a hedgehog, otter, dormouse, lizard and more. "Her love of the natural world had been life-long, and she would never leave home each year when fledgling jackdaws were about, as they would usually tumble down the sitting-room chimney and need to be released."[63] Once inspired by the bird life in the marshlands, and the animals and insects of the meadows and forests, she now became an avid viewer of TV natural history programmes, rivalled only by her love of sport. At 90 she was still happily sitting up till the early hours of the morning to watch cricket or snooker. The following day with her neighbours, Sally and Peter, who succeeded Dorothy Thorne in the adjoining cottage, she would always prefer to discuss the previous night's match rather than her health.[64]

(Top) Hedgehog, one of a series of small ceramic animals, modelled c. 1985; (above) Chailey village sign, designed by Marjorie shortly before her 90th birthday; (left) Sketch for "The Royal Oak" as seen on facing page.

ENID BLYTON AGAIN

In 1997, Marjorie's link with Enid Blyton was re-established when Sally photographed a model of Enid's home, Green Hedges, for Marjorie to use as the basis of a "doodle". Enid had been a keen supporter of Bekonscot Model Village, founded in aid of charity, in 1929, close to her home in Beaconsfield; and to mark the centenary of her birth the Village now added a one-twelfth-size scale model of Green Hedges and its garden.

Marjorie's resulting watercolour showed the little animals she used to illustrate for Enid creeping up to the model house wondering if Enid was inside writing about them. It was eagerly reproduced by Bekonscot's managers as a greetings card and put on sale at their shop to help raise funds for the Village and its charity.

Some months later, the Enid Blyton Society also made contact with Marjorie. Previously unaware that any of Enid's 'classic' illustrators were still alive, the society's editor, Tony Summerfield, who had made a study of Blyton's illustrators, arranged to visit her in 2000, bringing Enid's younger daughter, Imogen Smallwood. It was a red-letter day for Marjorie, and for them. As well as providing a first-hand insight into working for Enid, Marjorie produced her neat, handwritten workbook listing all the titles of the commissions, dates, medium used, date completed and despatched – and the fee she received. For the society's records it was an invaluable resource which they were grateful to borrow in order to update their archives, as many of her early illustrations were not signed.

In November the same year, the local museum at Ditchling, a few miles from Chailey, staged an exhibition of "Pictures by Marjorie Davies from the small world of Enid Blyton".[65] It was a display intended as a Christmas attraction for local children, but it drew considerable interest from local and regional media, including a full-page editorial in the *Evening Argus* and a mention on Southern Counties Radio. It also rated a brief item in the national news, when the *Daily Telegraph* included it in a round-up of forthcoming events for families, and reproduced Marjorie's "Cinder Paddocks" picture alongside illustrations by Quentin Blake, Beatrix Potter and Walter Crane.[66]

Opposite: "Do you think she is still in there writing about us?" (top) and Bekonscot Harbour, 1997.

This page: Ditchling Museum poster, 2000–1 and detail from "The Morris Mice visit Ditchling", reproduced by the museum as a postcard, 1998.

The exhibition gave Marjorie more than a little quiet satisfaction. And she was gratified to learn that while some of her "doodles" were being colour-copied in a nearby print-shop, they were noticed by local children's artist Raymond Briggs – author and illustrator of *The Snowman* – who remarked: "Now, that's the work of a trained artist."

Marjorie herself was not able to visit the exhibition, for by her 95th year she no longer felt safe walking outside her cottage or getting to and from a car; and had regretfully given up even the short ride each spring to see the new-born lambs at the farm on the hill where she used to work. Her weekly shopping and pension had, for some time, been delivered to her by the village shop. Her health checks were now carried out at home every month by the practice nurse, Mary Gent, who had become a dear friend and who broke all the rules by looking after Marjorie herself instead of assigning her home visits to the district nurses. Her major shopping and needs were seen to by her nieces, and friends and neighbours filled in the gaps with any urgent needs.

Pen–and-ink cover drawings for Chailey News: *(top) Chailey Place; (above) The Pump House; (right) Fonthill, 1990–2005.*

APPROACHING 100

Yet she was still preparing all her own meals, including a daily cooked lunch, though she had conceded that roasting half a chicken was easier to handle than a whole one. Her two cataract operations, in her 90s, gave her immense delight in the enhanced colours she could once again see and enjoy; and illustrating parish magazine covers became significantly easier. The pictures that had once been sketched on site, or from photos she herself had taken, were now, however, based on photos supplied by house owners or neighbours who went hunting for suitable subjects for her.

The covers formed a considerable collection and a unique village record, and in 2005 to support the work of Chailey Heritage for disabled children, she gave the enterprise unit at the Heritage the right to reproduce any of her cover drawings. It added to the interesting jobs the youngsters could undertake, raised money for the Heritage, and enabled local people to order mugs, table mats and coasters showing their own houses.

In preparation for her centenary year, Davydd Shaw wrote and published a personal memoir of her, *Marjorie Davies – an Appreciation*, drawing on her own recollections and including a remarkable, full-colour collection of her work spanning eighty years. She was particularly touched by the tribute, not least because she could refer local reporters to it when they wished to interview her, as they naturally did for her hundredth birthday.

Her nieces, meanwhile, made arrangements to celebrate the day, 5 June, 2006. "In her wisdom she has made us promise not to give her a party," they wrote to all her friends. "Although she is very well she feels it would

(Top) Pack Pony Lane; (above) Peter House; (left) Place mats and mugs produced by Chailey Heritage Enterprise Centre, 2005.

(Top) Ridgelands Bridge; (above) Honeysuckle Cottage.

be too much for her to cope with." Instead they invited contributions – photos, pictures, messages – to a 'box of treasures' which she could open at a small gathering of her immediate family and neighbours. "We will be toasting her birthday at 12 noon on 5th June and hope you will join us from across the miles." The messages and flowers she received gave her immense pleasure for weeks, as did all the greetings and cards sent to her again a year later.

Five months after her hundredth birthday she was still busy drawing covers for the parish magazine and wrote to the editor, who lived on Cinder Roughs: "I am getting woefully short of subjects. I think I have only drawn one cover from the Rough and there are so many super subjects, and I wondered if you could persuade your neighbours to lend me photos of their houses? I'd take great care of them and return them when I'd used them."

A few months later, however, she decided the time had come to retire, and her last cover appeared in June 2007, on her 101st birthday. The magazine, which had been continued by Eddie Matthias's successors, recorded the parish's debt to her:

"Once upon a time – so long ago that no one quite remembers when – Mrs Marjorie Davies drew her first pen-and-ink illustration for 'Chailey News'. Now she has decided that last month's picture, her own garden, should be her final cover. It is certainly more than 30 years since the first one appeared …

"It was not until January 1993, however, that she became our regular cover illustrator and since then, working from photographs supplied by friends and home-owners, she has produced a remarkable record of the buildings we all know and cherish … Some subjects were harder than others, but she never refused a challenge and never gave up on a picture that didn't quite 'work' – not even the notorious bridges sequence she was asked to draw in 1997.

"There are occasional breaks in the series, where the postal service or her health delayed the next drawing, and eagle-eyed readers will have spotted the odd 'reprise' that recently filled a gap. But there cannot be many parishes that have been privileged to receive a freshly drawn cover almost every month for 15 years. And surely none whose artist has decided to lay down her pen after her 101st birthday – in order to have more time for drawing children's 'doodles'!"

But a few months after her 101st birthday, Marjorie began to find living at home too much for her. It had been her wish to stay there, looking out on her garden, as long as she could, and with help she had managed to. At the end of August she spoke to Mary Gent, who immediately found her a respite room at the local nursing home, Nightingales, just a mile from her cottage.

Soon it became clear she would need to stay permanently but as there were no vacancies she gamely moved into a mobile home in the grounds, with Jacquie and the staff sharing the task of staying in it with her overnight. By day she might be found sitting laughing over memories with Mary Doherty, or Monica Hecks; chatting with family visitors and neighbours; or watching cricket on television, totally un-fazed by her odd surroundings.

(Above) Marjorie on her 100th birthday, June 2006.
(Right, top to bottom) Her last Christmas card, 2006;
an unfinished "doodle", June 2007; detail showing the
ladybird making a final appearance.

(Above): "The Timestone", drawn from her kitchen window, c. 2004; (below): Marjorie's obituary in the Independent.

When a permanent room became vacant she was moved back into the main house, but two months later, on 28 November, she died.

Marjorie's obituary in the *Independent* on 7 December occupied half a page and was accompanied by one of her cover illustrations for *Enid Blyton's Magazine*.

Her funeral at St Peter's parish church, on 10 December, was packed and so was the following lunch at the King's Head pub in North Chailey. Then a small group accompanied her coffin to Worth crematorium, and the following spring her ashes were placed under the "timestone" sundial in her garden.

APPENDIX 1

Enid Blyton's letters to M.L. Davies

Green Hedges,
Penn Road,
Beaconsfield,
Buckinghamshire
Jan. 25. 50

Dear Miss Davis [*sic*],

Thank you for your letter.

I am a very busy person, but if you like to send me a few of your drawings, both line and colour, I'll have a look at them. I hope you will not bother to send them unless you are pretty certain they are top-notch, as I use few artists who are not excellent at their job. It's a real plum to get an Enid Blyton book, as you know, and it's rare for a beginner to get a look in. Do not send enormous drawings, or a vast collection. I can tell at a glance from just a few whether your work is good and would suit me. Also, please send me your ordinary standard work – not wonderfully prepared "specimens".

Put in a stamped addressed return label with a sticky back, as all those details save my time. Send next week as I am a little less pressed for time then.

Yours sincerely,

Enid Blyton.

Have you an agent? If your work is good you should have one. I will recommend one if I think your work merits it.

Green Hedges …
Jan. 28. 50

Dear Mrs Davies,

Thank you for sending me your specimen drawings.

I like them all except for the Dew Star ones. Some of your colour work is excellent. I also like your animals, and you have a good child-like sense of humour.

I don't know if you'd like to ask for a story or two in my magazine 'Sunny Stories' (Geo. Newnes ltd.). The pay is not good, but the stories are good practice for anyone who wants to illustrate my work and sometimes eventually leads to a book commission.

I will give you introductions to 2 or 3 of my publishers, with a view to getting you one or two of my stories for illustration in my own annuals. I will enclose letters of introduction. You will realise that you will only be tried out at first with these publishers, and that it's entirely up to you to take advantage of the introductions by producing your very best work. I shall back you up if so, but not unless. I don't give introductions to many artists – only to about one in fifty, - so you will see that I really do consider you worth one!

Please be business like in your dealings with these publishers – keep to sizes mentioned, dates and so on, most meticulously. I do not like working with anyone slack in these matters – good work deserves a good business brain.

If you are thinking of leaving Link Studios, and feel you would like to deal with one that gets a lot of my work, I will put you in touch with one of the best as far as I am concerned. But if Link Studios get you plenty of work you had better stick to them.

I enclose letters of introduction. Go and see these publishers with your work if possible – write to them first of course, enclosing my letter of introduction – You will be able to see Brockhampton Press of course. They are a first-class children's publishing firm, affiliated to Hodders.

Yours sincerely,
Enid Blyton

P.T.O.

If I were you, I should suggest to these firms that if they give you a commission, you will be pleased to do the first one on the understanding that it's a try-out, and that if they dislike your work, or think it's not up to standard, they can reject it without payment. If you are certain of the standard of your work you can do this with the certainty 1) that it will make a good impression & 2) that it won't be rejected because it's too good for that!

Green Hedges …
Feb. 1. 50

Dear Mrs Davies,

Just to say that if you have definitely withdrawn your work from the Link, I would advise you to go and see – :

Mr. Penton, Byron Studios, 7 Carlisle Street, Soho Square, London.

Take a good selection of illustrations with you. He is an excellent agent, and if he likes your work, will certainly do his best for you. He will also be able to tell you when I am doing an annual, and probably give you a story or two. He has a great many contacts in the literary world.

I gave your name to one of my publishers the other day, and there is a possibility, that if one of the regular artists fails to accept the commission of a story or two, they might write to you. They are getting ready my "Second Bedside Book": the publisher is Arthur Barker, the printers (who may get in touch with you) are Morrison and Gibb.

Let me know what Mr. Penton says if you show him your work. I enclose a letter of introduction.

Yours sincerely,
Enid Blyton.

Green Hedges …
September 6, 59

Dear Mrs Davies,

What a wonderful surprise you gave me – & how very very generous of you! I was quite overcome when I saw the cheque and read your letter. Thank you more than I can say – for both. I am sad too that you and I will not be working together on my magazine any more – & I know you guess what a loss it is to me after all these years of being in such personal touch with my young and generous readers. But I did feel it would be selfish to go on now that my husband has retired – he has worked so very hard (as a consultant surgeon) and deserves to do all the things he loves doing – playing golf on his beloved golf-course (which he owns, & loves to plan alterations & so on for –

down in Dorset) & he loves his Dorset farm too – & I cannot let him do all these things alone – & yet cannot, of course, give up all my work for children – (he wouldn't want me to!) & so, as the magazine is the one thing that ties me down, & which has to go with me wherever I go (the work I mean!) I felt I must give it up. However the little *Busy Bees Magazine*, for which I write every month, will provide a link for me and my readers.

And now I must thank you for all your good (& most dependable work) and say that I hope this won't be the end of all collaboration! Your cheque will go into my Birthday Fund, & I will buy many birthday presents for the little ones in Home here in Beaconsfield. As you know, we take about 30, & you can guess the expenses we are always incurring! But somehow we survive – & now that Noddy is so much in demand in big Stores, for display purposes, I manage to get, at Christmas Time, quite a lot of gifts for them. I believe that Owen Owens in Liverpool are this year going to build a whole Noddy Village as a Christmas attraction – & all the money taken is to go to my little Home!

Well, I mustn't bore you – but I did feel I must say an extra big thank you to you for such a generous thought and gift – nothing could have pleased me more!

All the best to you,
Yours very sincerely
Enid Blyton

APPENDIX 2

Illustrations by M.L Davies for Enid Blyton

BOOKS

Second Bedside Book (published by Barker, Aug 1950)
    Michael's Tail
    A Mix Up
    Is Your Name Here?
    Riddle-Me-Ree
Buttercup Story Book (Gifford, Apr 51)
    When Tom Left the Tap On
    The Big Girl's Balloon
    He Didn't Like Animals
    Hidden Toys Puzzle
    Jim and Susan
    The Last Grunt
    Can You Do This?
Third Bedside Book (Barker, Aug 51)
    The Angry Wasp
    When Michael Missed the Bus
    The Mischievous Panda
    Hidden Flowers
    A Funny Little Puzzle
Sixth Holiday Book (Sampson Low, Sep 51)
    "I Was Here First!"
Snowdrop Story Book (Gifford, May 52)
    The Golliwogs' School

Wherever Can It Be?
Benny's Robin
The Strange Bicycle
Can You Guess Me?
Harry's New Football
Fourth Bedside Book (Barker, Jun 52)
    The Boy on the Bicycle
    One Snowy Night
    Billy-Up-The-Tree
    Who Comes Knocking at My Gate?
Enid Blyton Story Time Book (Purnell, 52)
    The Magic Lemonade
Water-Lily Story Book (Gifford, Jun 53)
    The Silly Little Cat
    Don't Cheat!
    When Sheila Ran Away!
    Poor Little Bear
    At the Seaside
    Riddle-Me-Ree
    An Exciting Afternoon
Fifth Bedside Book (Barker, Jul 53)
    The Christmas Pudding Wish
    Careless Connie
    Nobody's Friend

Eighth Holiday Book (Ampson Low, Sept 53)
  The Boy Who Never Put Things Back
Sixth Bedside Book (Barker, Jul 54)
  Endpapers
  Linda Loud-Voice
  Just One Thing After Another!
  The Day of the Party
  Let's Make Some Sweets
Marigold Story Book (Gifford, Jul 54)
  Johnny, Come at Once!
  He Didn't Want a Bath
  The Careless Kitten
  I Shall Sit Here
  This Will Puzzle You
  What Can it Be?
  How Good is Your Memory?
Seventh Bedside Book (Barker, Jul 55)
  Where's My Bicycle?
  The Way Things Go
  Sally's Sixpence
Foxglove Story Book (Gifford, Sep 55)
  Ladybird, Ladybird, Fly Away Home
  The Story That Came True
  Dan's Big Football
  A Seaside Puzzle
  Is Your Name Here?
Eighth Bedside Book (Barker, Jul 56)
  The Four-Leaved Clover
  The Hidden Doll
  Sally-Dog
  One Little Match
Ninth Bedside Book (Barker, Jul 57)
  Dustwrapper
  Next-Door James
  A Quarrelsome Morning
  What Would You Have Done?
  That Garden Gate!
  The New Tricycle
  My Baby Brother
  Half title page, title page, contents page
Tenth Bedside Book (Barker, Jul 58)
  Monkey Up a Tree
  I Shan't Speak to You!
  She Put in her Thumb
  The Eskimo Game
  Endpaper design
  You'd Better be Careful Pat
  Which am I?
  Swallows and Martins
  Puzzle of the Four Boys
  The Four-leaved Clover
  On Christmas night

Eleventh Bedside Book (Barker, Jul 59)
  Endpapers
  The Big Girl
  Umbrellas For the Dolls
  Crawler the Tortoise
  The Cat Did It!
  One Good Turn Deserves Another
  A Sea Song
  Can You Draw an Aeroplane?

MAGAZINES

Sunny Stories
Jun 50 A Letter from our Little Mouse
Jul 50 Boom-Diddy-Boom-Boom!
Aug 50 A Letter from Pinky
Sep 50 He Wanted to Smoke A Pipe
Dec 50 A Letter from Old Father time
Jan 51 Sailor Jim's Telescope
Jan 51 The Extraordinary Chair
Apr 51 Funny Little Mankie
Jun 51 The Bear in the Hall
Jul 51 A Tale of Two Boys – and a Kitten
Aug 51 How Silly
Sep 51 You Help Me and I'll Help You
Nov 51 It Grew and It Grew
Jan 52 White Trousers
Feb 52 Run, Noddy, Run!
    A Letter from Little Noddy
Mar 52 Well Done, Little Feet
    A Letter from Little Feet
Mar 52 What Are You Up to Now? (Cover)
May 52 Buttercup Magic
July 52 Well Done, Kite!
Sept 52 Where's my Tail?
    A Letter from Bun
Nov 52 He Forgot His Dog
    A Letter from Benny
Dec 52 A Hat for Little Bear
(MLD continued illustrating for the new editors of
Sunny Stories from Jan to Nov 1953)

Enid Blyton's Magazine
Mar 53 The Ship in the Bottle (Cover)
Apr 53 Gobble-Gobble-Gobble
June 53 When Bessie Flew the Kite
June 53 It Wasn't his Fault (Cover)
Sep 53 Lennie's Little Trick
Jan 54 Peculiar Happenings (Cover)
Apr 54 A Ribbon in the Sky (Cover)
May 54 They Made Some Mud
(date?) A Letter from Sarah

Sep 54 Think a Bit Harder, Simon!
Sep 54 The Little Tease
Oct 54 Bonfire Night is Coming!
Oct 54 A letter from David
Dec 54 Little Pig, Come Here!
Jan 55 Here You Are, Squirrel!
Feb 55 She Didn't Catch the Bus! (Cover)
Mar 55 The Two Money-Boxes
May 55 You Never Know What Will Turn Up
Aug 55 Well Done, Santa!
Oct 55 Who has Won?
Oct 55 How Dare You?
Jan 56 Is There Anything Particular you Want?
Feb 56 At Granny's
Feb 56 The Big Humming Top
July 56 Anyone would do the same
Aug 56 A Jigsaw Lesson
Oct 56 Something Went Wrong!
Dec 56 A Surprise for Henry
Jan 57 George Has a Bit of Fun

Mar 57 Here Comes the Tiddler!
Jul 57 Wake Up, Grandpa!
Oct 57 Harry's Fine Idea
Dec 57 Come On, Wags!
Feb 58 The Jumble-Puppy
Mar 58 The Spaniel and the Robin
Apr 58 Well of All the Peculiar Things (Cover)
Jun 58 What a Piece of Luck! (Cover)
Jul 58 What a Good Idea, Graham! (Cover)
Nov 58 The Ugly Little Dog (Cover)
Mar 59 A Real Bit of Luck! (Cover)
Jun 59 A Dog Called Timmy (1) (Cover)
Sep 59 A Dog Called Timmy (2) (Cover)

Other possible work for *Enid Blyton's Magazine:*
(undated) Where did you get them from, Dave?
(undated) Robin and his Dog
Jun 56 The Buttercup Spell
Dec 57 You'd Better be Careful Stamp-About
May 58 A Pins and Needles Spell

NOTES

1 Alfred Clements was born on 15 October, 1871; Louise (*née* Agnes Louisa Tomlinson) on 4 September, 1873; John Clements in 1857, and Bert (Bertie) Clements in 1881.

2 Jacquie Bravery to SV: Jack (Alfred John Tomlinson Clements) was born 11 May, 1902; Eric in June 1904; Con (Conway Mellor Clements) on 19 May, 1908; Vic (Charles Victor Clements) on 12 May, 1912.

3 MLD to SV, 1980s. Louise died at The Home Sanatorium on 5 February, 1924.

4 Davydd Shaw to SV: William and Doris's mother, Elizabeth (died c1906), was another of Alfred's sisters. Their father, Samuel Gent, remarried c1913/14 and had six more children. Will, according to his son John Gent: "Once said he'd have liked to marry Marjorie, if she hadn't been his cousin."

5 DS to SV: "My grandfather, George Clements, was Alfred Clements's youngest brother. George emigrated to Australia in 1887 with another brother, William, and their father, by then a widower."

6 DS to SV. This visit may well have taken place early in 1924, after Marjorie left school and before Alfred remarried in April 1925.

7 MLD to Enid Blyton's daughter Imogen Smallwood, 2000.

8 Mabel Alice Kell was born 14 May, 1876.

9 MLD to DS.

10 MLD to SV.

11 DS to SV: "Following Alfred's death, Maggie became housekeeper to Marjorie's cousin Wally (Walter) Forster around the mid-1950s, after the death of his wife, Elsie. Walter lived at Wembley and retired to Shanklin, where he died in 1968. Maggie then retired to the north of England but often visited Marjorie in the 1970s." John Gent also recalled the family's fondness for Maggie and her visits to his parents in Croydon in the late 1960s.

12 Davydd Shaw., *Marjorie Davies: An Appreciation*, 2005, ISBN 0-646-44697-5

13 MLD to SV.

14 MLD to SV.

15 The comic strip had first appeared in the *Daily Mirror* in May, 1919. Though Marjorie worked on one of the "Pip, Squeak and Wilfrid" annuals, she does not

appear to have been commissioned to produce any of the newspaper strips.

16 MLD to IS, 2000.

17 MLD to SV.

18 DS to SV: "Marjorie considered Violet Wilson a good artist, whose landscapes and subjects were nearly always of a gloomy or mysterious nature – I have one such example in B&W. Violet loved the moors and the relative isolation of their cottage on the road up to Dartmoor, on the edge of Mary Tavy." While some found Violet occasionally discouraged visiting, Angie Clements Jenkins recalled: "Auntie Vee and I used to write to each other regularly. I think she was just very private, like Auntie Marjorie, rather than unsociable. Her watercolours were strong, full of intricate detail. Quite 'dark' in many ways (almost pagan). They were beautiful."

19 MLD to DS.

20 MLD to SV; the year is confirmed by John's indentures.

21 A copy of *Rivers and Creeks of the Thames Estuary* kept among John's books was inscribed H. J. Davies.

22 MLD to SV. One address for him in MLD's early address book is: St Alphage House, 45 Aldbermanbury, EC2. This is not close enough to St Paul's to be his office address at the time of the Blitz.

23 MLD to SV.

24 For the rest of Marjorie's life, John's attic work-room, full of his tools and workbench, with the floor almost ankle-deep in off-cuts of furniture and broken china, remained almost untouched.

25 DS, *An Appreciation*.

26 MLD to DS.

27 MLD to SV.

28 JB and John Gent to SV.

29 MLD to SV.

30 MLD to SV.

31 *DS, An Appreciation*.

32 The letter continues: " Will you arrange to travel on Monday, May 11th to the East Sussex County Office, Castle Place, Lewes (Tel. Lewes 446) arriving as soon after 10.30 a.m. as possible. The County Secretary, Mrs.

Lowman, will then arrange for you to be conveyed to Peacehaven with the other volunteers. I shall be transferring your papers to Mrs Lowman with whom you should always get in touch if in any difficulty. I enclose a travelling voucher and wish you all success. Yours sincerely, Susannah Sharp, County Secretary."

33 Mary Doherty (1921 – 2010) to SV.

34 In her funeral eulogy they wrote: "She thoroughly enjoyed the companionship of 20 other girls in the hostel ... [and she] ... remained friends with most of the girls for the rest of her life. The work was extremely hard and arduous ... Corn stacks and haystacks needed a thatched roof to keep them dry so Mary became an expert at thatching. On at least one occasion the haystacks had to be rebuilt after [her brother] Bernard flew his Hurricane fighter plane down so low that it blew the haystacks down. In the evenings they were often invited to dances by the local soldiers and airmen, this sometimes involved climbing out of the window at the hostel and getting lifts with eight others in a car ... Perhaps it was after work or from one of these dances that cycling back to the hostel one night Mary crashed into a cow that was standing in the road... Not even a Doodle Bug crashing in the next field seemed to distract her from her adventures in the Land Army... [in a poem about the Land Army] ... she describes how she came to 'love the land' and how she felt she would never leave it ... the Land Army and the war were to shape [her] for the rest of her life."

35 DS, *An Appreciation*.

36 Mary Doherty to SV.

37 In some correspondence her address is given as Fruit Farm Bungalow.

38 The letters, transcribed in full at Appendix 1, were discovered by JB and ACJ among MLD's papers after her death.

39 The 10 drawings for "Michael's Tail", plus the three one-page items earned MLD a total of £30.9s.0d.

40 Imogen Smallwood and Tony Summerfield, writing in *The Enid Blyton Society Journal*, winter 2000, recorded what MLD had told them when they visited her earlier in 2000: "In the late 1940s ... she began to send her work around. Mr Penton of the Byron Studios, which she had joined at this time, was discouraging. He told her that she had left it too long after coming out of the Land Army because the men were now back

from the war and taking all the jobs. But she persevered and eventually, as a last resort, wrote to Enid Blyton to ask if she could send her some illustrations. Enid, as is well known, was an excellent and reliable correspondent. She replied to Marjorie's letter, inviting her to send some work, 'only if it is first class'. So, very sensibly, Marjorie sent the drawings and Enid was delighted with them. Very soon Enid began to send some of her work direct to Marjorie for illustration and the pessimistic Penton was then reduced to the role of go-between."

41 A complete list of MLD's work for Enid Blyton (not all of it signed, but witnessed by her account books) appears at Appendix 2.

42 Smallwood and Summerfield, *The Enid Blyton Society Journal*, as above.

43 TS to SV, 2010.

44 MLD to DS.

45 JB to SV: "I think at one time he ran away and joined a circus! I remember him living with us for quite a long time when I was very young." DS remembered, on a visit to Vic and Anne with Marjorie, in 1979: "Vic was obviously pleased to show me his well-equipped workshop on site where he was skilled in wood and metal work. In World War II he served in the Air Force, where he was a member of a mechanics crew."

46 MLD to SV.

47 Mr Spicer had occupied Number 1 from before 1933, though it was bought in 1949 by his daughter, Dorothy and her husband Charles Thorne. As Charlie witnessed John and Marjorie's signatures on 7 May, 1954, the Thornes were obviously already living there with Mr Spicer.

48 Graves, Son & Pilcher to MLD, 5 March, 1954.

49 D.W. Wilkins, Newick.

50 C. Beard & Son, South Chailey.

51 MLD to Peter Varlow.

52 MLD to PV.

53 In 2010 ACJ recalled sleeping in the room as a child with her sisters in the 1950s; "on a large mattress on the floor". It is possible the mattress was later replaced with beds, as JB recalled: "I used to sleep in the bed on the right-hand side of the studio and Gilly and Angie shared the left bed – I remember that so clearly as when I got out of bed I would lurch towards theirs due to the slope of the bedroom floor!" By 1982, all beds and mattresses had gone and the Studio was filled with MLD's artworks and easel.

54 MLD to DS.

55 The suggestion that the subject of the request was *The Secret Seven* was made by Tony Summerfield to SV, 2010.

56 Copies of painting books kept with her sketchbooks, *The Good Artist's Painting Book*; *Our Painting Book*; *Little Pets Painting and Tracing Book* (Dean & son); *Party Time Painting Book* (Birn Bros); and *Mystery Painting Book*, may contain her work, but may also be samples sent to her by the Link.

57 MLD to SV.

58 MLD to SV; confirmed by DS.

59 MLD to SV, 2004: "John lost his job when he was 67". That cannot be quite correct as he would not have reached 67 until April 1968. His death certificate described him as: Antiques Dealer's Assistant (retired).

60 Charlie Thorne died 1962.

61 John Seabrook in conversation with SV at Plumpton College.

62 MLD to SV.

63 DS, *An Appreciation*.

64 Source: PV. Sally and Peter Varlow bought No 1 Coppard's Bridge after Dorothy Thorne died, 1981.

65 Ditchling Museum, Church Lane, Ditchling; 4 November, 2000 to 7 January, 2001.

66 The *Evening Argus*, 11 November, 2000; Southern Counties Radio, 24 November, 2000; the *Daily Telegraph*, 30 September, 2000.